The Pleasures of Knitting

The Pleasures of Knitting

Martingale®
& COMPANY

Timeless Feminine Sweaters

Ann McCauley

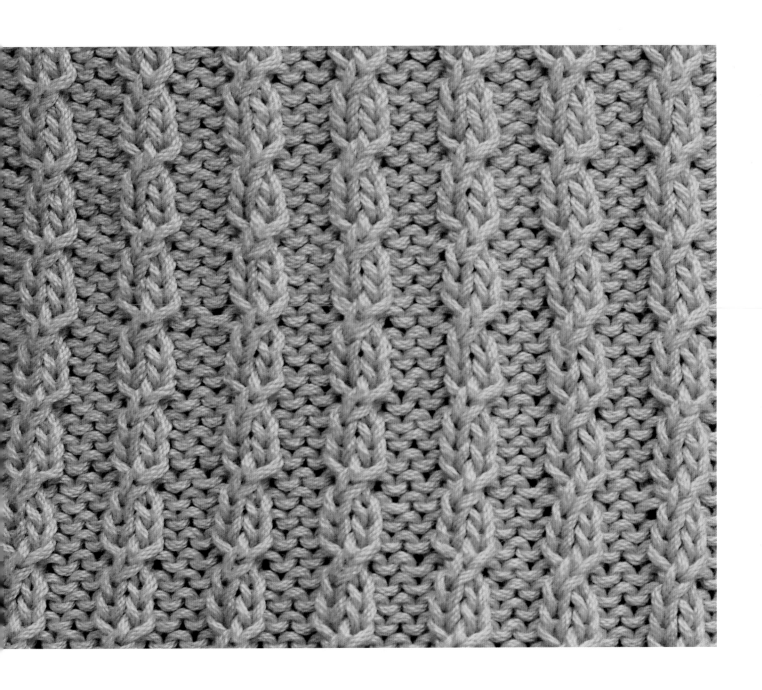

Credits

President	Nancy J. Martin
CEO	Daniel J. Martin
Publisher	Jane Hamada
Editorial Director	Mary V. Green
Managing Editor	Tina Cook
Technical Editor	Ursula Reikes
Copy Editor	Ellen Balstad
Design Director	Stan Green
Illustrator	Robin Strobel
Cover Designer	Stan Green
Text Designer	Trina Craig
Model Photographer	J.P. Hamel
Fashion Stylist	Susan Huxley
Studio Photographer	Brent Kane

Martingale & Company
20205 144th Avenue NE
Woodinville, WA 98072-8478 USA
www.martingale-pub.com

The Pleasures of Knitting: Timeless Feminine Sweaters
© 2005 by Ann McCauley

Printed in China
10 09 08 07 06 05   8 7 6 5 4 3 2 1

Mission Statement

Dedicated to providing quality products and service to inspire creativity.

Library of Congress Cataloging-in-Publication Data

McCauley, Ann.
    The pleasures of knitting : timeless feminine sweaters / Ann McCauley.
        p. cm.
    Includes bibliographical references.
    ISBN 1-56477-566-6
    1. Knitting–Patterns.   2. Sweaters.   I. Title.
    TT825.M384 2005
    746.43'20432–dc22

2004020680

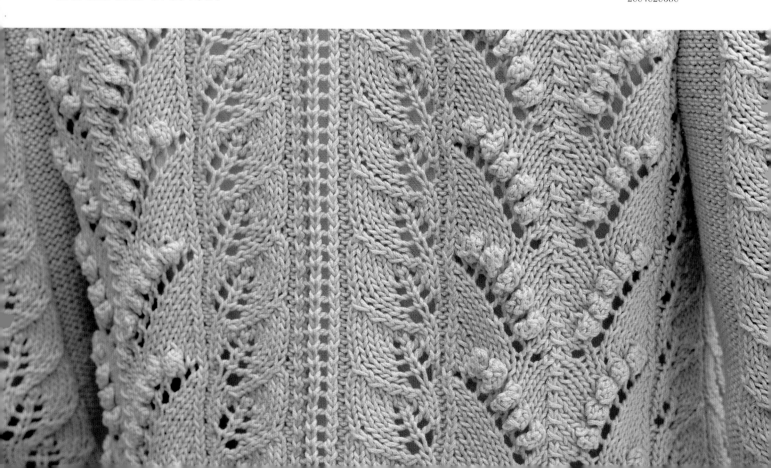

Dedication

To all knitters and the immediate bond that exists among those who love the art of hand knitting.

Acknowledgments

I would like to acknowledge and express heartfelt thanks to all who have encouraged me in this pursuit, from my closest loved ones, family, and friends, to those I haven't known personally but who took the time to say, "I love that sweater you're wearing. Where did you get it?"

I would also like to express my sincerest gratitude to the staff of Martingale & Company for their enthusiasm and support for this project.

contents

My strongest passions are dancing and knitting. I knew this as a child. I think I was around nine years old when I observed my mother knitting and I said to her, "I want to do that!" In no time I had beautiful wooden knitting needles with red spheres on the ends in my hands. I made headbands from knit strips. I found a slipper pattern and immediately made slippers for half a dozen people in the family. I said to my mother, "I love this! I want to make a sweater." My mother said, "You'll never finish a sweater." Of course, what my mother meant was that it took her a really long time to finish a sweater. At this early age, I already knew that sweaters were my favorite things to wear.

My knitting desire was put on hold until I became an adult and began to travel to Europe on tour with a modern dance company. I saw people knitting everywhere. And there was that clear voice and strong impulse once again saying "I want to do that! I want to make a sweater." This time there was no stopping me, and I have to think that that voice was actually the beginning of this book.

My hands may have temporarily forgotten how to knit, but it wasn't for long. The patterns on the following pages are part of what ensued, as well as many hours of knitting and discovering that this expression is as much a meditation and creation as dance. I discovered that, oddly enough, there is an amazing overlap between dancing and knitting, and that dancing actually informs knitting on a conceptual level. Pattern, form, design, repetition, kinesthetic awareness, movement skills, creativity—these elements of dance and more constantly inform my work as a knitter.

I believe the act of knitting integrates body, mind, and spirit. The physical and sensory level is primarily tactile, visual, and kinesthetic in nature. For the mind, it can bring meditative space and a positive influence for memory. And for our spiritual beings, there is creativity, imagination, and visualization.

I feel that the creative arts, the performing arts, and the healing arts must be accessible to as many as possible if we are to achieve some of the positive changes we would all like to see in our world. I know that knitting has been a healing activity for me, and as our hands touch and form our knitting, in turn our knitting touches others. I know that the sweaters in this book have been deeply satisfying for me to discover and create. I truly hope that you enjoy making and wearing these sweaters as much as I have.

Alphabet of Tips from A to Z

These tips apply to every design in *The Pleasures of Knitting* and are most helpful to read before making these sweaters.

a

awareness

A simple knitter's pleasure is having that perfect spot in which we love to knit. Yes, we may knit on the go, but when we knit at home, physical comfort is a significant aspect of our knitting. How we use our bodies influences not only our knitting but also how we feel. We are energetic beings, and when energy is moving freely through our body, we feel good. When energy is not moving through some part, such as a shoulder, lower back, knee, or hand, we feel stiff, tight, achy, or congested. Awareness grants us the ability to acknowledge and change things that are not moving. Our ability to pay attention and to be in the present enhances awareness.

alignment

With basic awareness of optimal alignment and body mechanics, we can knit with greater ease. When we stand, we have the opportunity to align our bodies vertically in space for greater balance and energy. When we sit, our *ischial tuberoscity* (which will be referred to informally as our *sit bones* from this point forward since we sit on them, and we're usually sitting when we're knitting) become the equivalent of what our feet are when we are standing. Let me explain.

We have the ability to center ourselves, and if we pay attention to our bodies, they will tell us what we need to know. When we are sitting, it is optimal if the soles of our feet are on the floor; it helps to ground us. Whether we are standing, sitting, or walking, it is helpful to feel the prints that the soles of our feet make against the ground. When we sit, large contemporary furniture does not always afford us that opportunity unless we put a pillow behind our backs, which brings us forward and allows our feet to reach the ground. A small pillow behind the lower back will help support the curve in the lumbar spine for a knitter whose lower back feels tight or fatigued after sitting for a while. Our spines are meant to have an elongated S-shaped curve for optimal functioning. When we are standing, sitting, or walking with a clear vertical orientation, a sense of order around our own verticality, we can allow the optimal S curve to occur. We have the ability to organize our structures vertically in space.

To align your pelvis vertically in space, sit with your weight on top of your sit bones. If you sit with your weight behind your sit bones, your pelvis will be tilted back or tucked under, and you may experience less energy and comfort.

Vertical Supportive Alignment

Tilted Pelvis; Less Supportive Alignment

You can encourage awareness of the sit bones by sitting in a kneeling position with your heels pressing in front of the sit bones. Or, if you find yourself growing weary while sitting in a chair, simply slide your hands underneath you and sit with your fingers pressing in front of the sit bones for a moment.

Kneeling Position   Sitting on Hands

b

body mechanics

Since movement patterns are so often habitual, I know it is hard not to cross your legs if you're used to it. However, when we cross our legs, we diminish circulation in our legs, which will eventually contribute to what are commonly known as spider veins.

When we sit vertically rather than slumping or leaning, the upper body is balanced over the pelvis, and the shoulders, neck, and head can feel more support. As we knit, we need to periodically notice whether our shoulders are relaxed. If there is tension, try the following options:

✦ Allow your shoulders to drop and soften as you exhale fully.

✦ Use your hand to gently squeeze the top of your shoulder.

✦ Feel the weight of your elbows. Letting the elbows be heavy helps to release the top of the shoulders.
✦ Move the elbows to a position in which they are wider than the shoulders, which can encourage a more open feeling across the upper back.
✦ Reach with your fingers into the spaces between the ribs and just off the outer edge of the shoulder blade along the side seam from the armpit down, and rub vigorously there.

Knitters may benefit from resting an elbow on the arm of a chair or sofa if it is at the right height. When you knit with circular needles, a pillow in your lap may increase the comfort level for the neck and shoulders, as well as the arms and hands, by bringing the work a little closer to eye level. Find the support and angles that feel best for the structure and proportions of your body. Just like our sweater, we hope to create a lovely fit.

If your head gets heavy or your neck gets tight, it's telling you it wants to move. Your neck wants to feel that natural curve where it is most comfortable. Dropping your head forward over your work pulls that curve out. And moving back toward vertical will support you.

You will find more about hands under *G* and *H*.

blocking

Blocking is a step of finishing not to be overlooked and the key to a garment's final appearance. Meticulous blocking enhances your knitting and makes your finished garment more beautiful. It involves steaming your garment to even out stitching lines and yarn fibers, since many stitches or patterns require opening up and evening out. This is especially true of sweaters with lots of texture, whether there are lacy, open stitches or multiple cables.

I like to block on the floor. I use a very thick towel and put it down on top of carpet. If you can find a towel that has a pattern on it resembling graph paper, or even one with larger squares or lines, it can be a helpful guideline. Begin by pinning your garment pieces to the towel. Lay the work down flat and smooth. Straighten and open the stitches as you pin down the edges; use lots of pins. Pin every ¼" to ½", depending on the pattern. Nice edges make nice seams. I like to pin both the back and front pieces at the same time and both sleeves at the same time to ensure accurate measurements and symmetry. Once you think you have the pieces pinned and shaped to perfection, walk away and take a break so that you can come back to the project later with a fresh eye for that last check. This is important, and I almost always notice some tiny detail in this last step before steaming.

To steam, simply fill an iron with water and preheat it. Cover the work to be blocked with a clean linen tea towel. With a spray bottle of water, dampen the tea towel. Then hold the iron lightly on the damp towel without pressure, and steam iron each area of the work evenly. Be sure not to miss edges. If you use long pins with a bead-type round head for pinning, you will feel where the edges are. I leave the piece or pieces pinned down overnight for thorough drying. The only sweater in this book that is not blocked as a design choice is Flair Mock Cable Pullover on page 61 because it is the only design that you do not want to open up and stretch out.

C

casting on

Cable cast on is undisputably my preferred way to cast on. It produces a nice edge. The only difference in the cable cast on and knit cast on is that instead of inserting the right-hand needle into the stitch to make the next stitch, you insert it between two stitches.

Wrap yarn around the right needle and pull through to make a stitch.

Place the new stitch on the left needle.

I use the knit cast on for working sleeve increases as in the Vertical Rib Pullover on page 26, and the Stripes and Web Boatneck on page 42.

Knit into the first stitch on the left needle. Do not drop the stitch off.

Place the new stitch on the left needle.

color

Choose colors that you love to wear. If there's a color you love, chances are you already own something in that color. Take that item with you when you shop for yarn. If it's a color you haven't worn, find a mirror and hold a few skeins near your face in good light to determine if it's right for you.

creativity

The creative spirit nurtures the soul. Allow your creativity full and free range.

d

decreases

In working single decreases, I use K2tog tbl or SSK at the beginning of the row and K2tog at the end of the row on RS rows regardless of stitch patterns. On a WS row, I use P2tog tbl or SSP at the beginning of the row and P2tog at the end of the row so that the bumps the purl stitches create are on the WS of the knitting. Remember that these decreased stitches will end up in a seam. I prefer the seam edge to be as smooth as possible.

In working decreases on curved or tapered edges such as shaping armholes, sleeve caps or shoulders, and certain types of necklines, my method is slightly different for binding off the subsequent rows after the initial row. I use a normal bind off for the initial bind off row to define the edge. Then for all following rows with stitches to be bound off, I choose to work the first two stitches together (as in K2tog tbl or P2tog tbl) and pass that over the next stitch before continuing to bind off the instructed number of stitches. Working the first two stitches together produces a smoother curved edge and

less of a bump or step than binding off the first stitch in the normal manner. I believe this promotes better seaming and a smoother neckline.

Here's an example of standard directions for armhole shaping:

+ BO 3 sts at beg of next 2 rows.
+ BO 2 sts at beg of next 2 rows.
+ BO 1 st at beg of next 2 rows.

In this book, the above directions for armhole shaping are written as follows:

+ BO 3 sts at beg of next 2 rows.
+ Dec 1 st, then BO 1 st at beg of next 2 rows.
+ Dec 1 st at beg of next 2 rows.

As you can see the first set of bind offs (BO 3) are the same for each set of directions. I would BO 3 sts kw, assuming that this is a RS row, and then BO 3 sts pw, assuming that this is a WS row. The difference between the standard method and my method occurs at the beginning of the next 2 rows. On a RS row, I work K2tog tbl (1 st is gone), K1 and pass the K2tog tbl st over the K1 (2 sts are gone). On a WS row, I work P2tog tbl, P1, and pass the P2tog tbl st over the P1. For the final 2 rows, I would simply K2tog tbl or P2tog tbl.

e

enthusiasm

Share your enthusiasm for what you know and love. Teach others to knit. It will be a great gift to many.

f

fit

You will be happiest with your hand-knit sweaters if you personalize their fit. As we know, bodies come in more than three or four sizes. Proportions vary. For example, some people like their sleeves longer than others. Check the measurements of each piece of a garment against your own body to make sure it works for you. It is usually not too complex to add or subtract a few rows or stitches so that the investment of your time, energy, and creativity will be appropriately rewarded with the fit you desire. If it is more convenient to measure a sweater that you wear and love than to measure your own body, do it. Note that neck length is highly variable. For example, to find the length that is most flattering in a turtleneck style, measure the length of a turtleneck you wear and like. This will save you time and prevent you from having to go back and unravel stitches or add on.

folding

When folding sweaters for storage on closet shelves or in drawers, I like to lay the sweater front down on a flat surface, fold the wrist of a sleeve to the opposite shoulder and repeat for the other side, and then fold the sweater in half from bottom to top. Never store sweaters on hangers unless you are using a pant hanger or a hanger with some padding across the lower edge, and then you must fold the sweater horizontally over that edge. Sleeves should not dangle and must be folded over the hanger edge, resting on top of the body of the sweater. Sweaters may also be folded in half vertically, which works nicely for unbuttoned cardigans, and then draped horizontally over the hanger with the sleeves resting on top of the front of the sweater. If you do not have appropriate hangers, you can drape a hand towel over the lower edge of a wire hanger.

g

gauge

Checking gauge is another imperative piece to making a sweater that is wonderful. In all of the patterns in the book except for Flair Mock Cable Pullover on page 61, the gauge given is the gauge of the piece *when it is blocked.* Therefore, when checking the gauge of a swatch, you can leave the swatch on the needle, pin it down as if you were going to block it, and count your stitches and rows per inch over several inches.

Gauge is a reflection of the tension we use in our hands as we move them while holding the needles and the yarn. This is another place where we are looking for ease of motion, flow, fluidity, and rhythm. We don't want the stitches too tight and we don't want them too loose. Optimally stitches slide easily. This can be an area that challenges the new knitter until the movement of how to knit is processed by the body. Give this time to happen and familiarity will assist.

h

hands

There is tremendous energy and life force in the human hand. Our hands can be utilized therapeutically, such as with touch, and creatively, such as with knitting. There are simple exercises we can do to support the use of the hands, to increase the sensitivity of the hands, to reduce stress and fatigue in the hands, and simply to promote a sense of balance in the body because we know that nothing that happens in our bodies is an isolated or localized event. The natural state of the body is to function in harmony. Three simple exercises are given below for you to practice. These can be done at any time in the day but are particularly useful when you awaken in the morning or before you fall asleep, and before you begin to knit or when you finish knitting.

holding fingers

We can do something this simple to help ourselves on many levels. Simply wrap the fingers of one hand around the little finger of your other hand, just as an infant would. Hold the little finger as long as you feel drawn to do so. You may feel a pulse or some movement in the little finger after a while. When you do, or when you feel ready to move on, hold the ring finger. Continue this process until you have held each finger sequentially, finishing with the thumb.

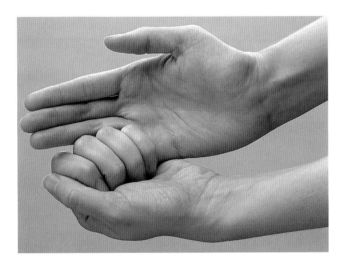

After holding the thumb, reach across the web between the index finger and the thumb so that the thumb of the opposite hand is resting in the palm-side center of the receiving hand. You may notice a difference in the way your two hands feel. Then change hands and repeat for the other hand. As you practice this, go beyond holding and work a little more deeply if you feel inclined.

It can be supportive and beneficial to reach with the tips of the thumb and index finger of one hand into the lower joint of the finger underneath where a ring would be on the opposite hand. Simply hold or massage this area using gentle and/or firm pressure as you prefer.

fingertip circles

Bring the very tip of your thumb and little finger on the same hand to touch (one hand or both simultaneously), making a circle. Hold this position as long as you desire, for a few seconds or longer, until you feel a pulse or some movement. Sequentially continue making that circle with the thumb and ring finger, then thumb and middle finger, and finally thumb and index finger.

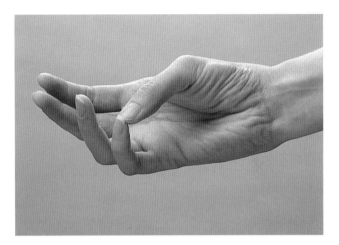

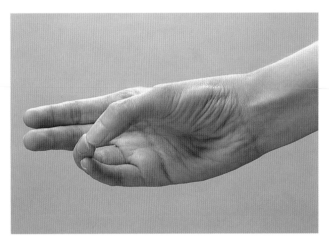

wrist-to-fingertip lines

With your thumb on the palm side of your wrist and your index finger on the back of your hand, and using some pressure, slide the thumb and index finger from the base of your wrist down the hand and down the little finger, inching along and off the tip of the finger two or more times. Repeat this for the ring finger, middle finger, index finger, and thumb. Most people find it more comfortable to rotate the hand so that the thumb is on the back of the hand and the index finger is on the palm side of the hand before they repeat this movement down the index finger and thumb.

Enjoy the way your hands feel—articulate, supple, fluid, open, and expressive.

i

I-cord

I-cord is a useful trim or edging. Attached I-cord is used at the neckline of Peri's Parasol Pullover on page 47 and the front edges of Lily of the Valley Cardigan on page 90. I-cord is a small tube of stockinette stitch made with two double-pointed needles. To work attached I-cord, follow these steps:

1. Pick up stitches along area (neckline, edge) where you wish to attach I-cord.

2. Using two double-pointed needles and separate ball of yarn, cast on desired number of stitches.

3. Slip one stitch from picked up stitches on garment to end of the row of stitches on double-pointed needle, knit to last two stitches, and then knit those stitches together through back loop.

4. Do not turn work, slide stitches to opposite end of needle, and repeat step 3.

5. Repeat steps 3 and 4 until all stitches are worked and bound off. Sliding the stitches to the opposite end of the needle as in step 4 creates a sort of ladder up the back of the work that, when gently stretched, creates the tube.

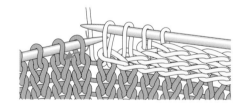

inspiration

Let your knitting be inspired by the world around you, with its many colors, shapes, and choices. Allow the sensitivity that knitting awakens in your hands to enhance your quality of touch toward those that surround you.

j

journal

A journal is a very handy tool for a knitter. It's a place to record the sizes and types of needles you have, the yarn you have, yarn labels, dye lots, washing instructions, measurements, how you may have altered a pattern in case you want to make it again, and any information that is helpful to you as a knitter. *The Pleasures of Knitting* would never have come into existence if there hadn't been a knitting journal first.

k

knitting

Knitting is a gift, both the process and the product. One of the greatest gifts for me is that it eliminates something from my life that I am not very good at—waiting. You are never waiting if you have your knitting with you. And knitting is the only way I can rationalize having the television on.

knowing

Know what you like and knit it so that you will wear and enjoy it.

l

lace stitches

Lace stitches are open, light, and airy, and are usually produced by yarn overs. They are wonderful for those who live in warmer climates. Also, do not hesitate to use lace stitches in wool for an "air-conditioned" or "midlife" sweater. Lace stitches also create beautiful scarves and shawls.

light

I know it seems like a simple and obvious thing, but please be certain that you knit in a well-lit spot. Your eyes will thank you, and it will minimize fatigue. Remember to be especially aware of this when knitting with black or dark yarns.

m

measuring

As discussed relative to fit, measuring is an essential part of ensuring a good result and the measurements must be accurate. To be certain about a gauge measurement, you can always pin your work down as if to block it while it is still on the needle and measure it.

It is helpful to know that the finished bust measurements at the beginning of the sweater patterns reflect the width around the entire sweater at the underarm. For example, if you know you are a 32" bust and wear a size Small and the pattern you wish to make lists 35" as the bust measurement for your size, then you know that your sweater will have 3" of ease around the bust. Ease is a term for the amount of extra room you'll have when you wear your sweater. Ease will indicate to you how closely or loosely fitting your sweater will be. It is best to determine your bust measurement with a tape measure and not assume it from your bra size, as the cup size of your bra will also be a factor.

movement

As you knit, sense the movement of your knitting passing through the center of your joints, particularly the shoulders, elbows, and wrists, and even the smaller joints of the fingers. Recognize all of the smaller-scale movements or intrinsic movement in the body as you knit. It will help keep your body open and alleviate tension or fatigue.

n

needles

There are different types of needles for different purposes. Essentially your needles will be straight, circular, or double pointed. Different sizes and lengths will be required. I like to buy good needles because they last longer and function better. Needles are made of wood, metal, plastic, or other newer materials, and you will have to go through a process of discovering what works and feels best for you. Store needles so that they will not be damaged. If needles become bent or warped, or if you wear the tips away, replace them.

o

original

Never be afraid to make something up on your own and create an original project. If at first you don't succeed, you can simply start over and try again.

p

process and product

When you engage in a process, you take all the steps that lead you to a finished product, which in this context is a beautiful hand-knit garment to wear and treasure for many years. Enjoy both these aspects of knitting.

q

quintessential

Quintessential describes the purest essence of something existing in the present moment, which in turn reflects the meditative quality many knitters enjoy from the orderly, repetitive activity of knitting.

r

resilience

Resilience is a word that accurately describes a quality that knit garments and our bodies and spirits possess. It is one of the qualities that makes knit garments so appealing to wear. In the words of Will Johnson, from his book *The Posture of Meditation: A Practical Guide for Meditators of All Traditions,* "Resilience is the quality that nurtures the conditions of alignment and relaxation and extends their presence over time."

rhythm

Let your hands find a rhythm as you knit. This may not happen until you are a few rows into your work, but it will be there for you and allow your work to flow. The body loves rhythm and is filled with it.

row counter

A row counter is an extremely useful tool to help keep track of what row you're on, particularly for the Vertical Rib Pullover on page 26. It is a small device that can fit on the top of your knitting needle or sit on a table beside you. As you finish a row, you manually change the number on the counter. I also believe that with mindfulness, you can cultivate the ability to remember what row you are on.

S

seaming

Different seaming techniques are appropriate for different areas in a garment. They do make the difference in a professional-looking garment. Work all seaming techniques with the right side of the work facing you, and secure the tail at the end of the seam. If done carefully and inconspicuously, I am not opposed to securing the tail with a knot, although many "dyed in the wool" knitters are and believe you should simply weave the tail securely into the work without knotting.

Weave the tail into the wrong side of the garment vertically using a yarn needle or crochet hook. If you weave a tail in horizontally, you will create a ridge.

beginning seaming

The way to begin seaming is with a figure eight. Use a long tail (about 18") from a cast-on row to thread your yarn needle. With the right sides of pieces to be seamed facing you, insert the yarn needle from back to front into the corner stitch of the work without the tail. You will then make a figure eight with the tail, which might be more accurately described as the infinity sign, since the eight is lying on its side. Insert the needle from back to front into the stitch with the cast-on tail.

Gently tighten or secure to close the beginning of the seam.

invisible horizontal for shoulders

Line up the bound-off edges stitch for stitch. Insert the yarn needle under a stitch inside the bound-off edge of one side and under the corresponding stitch on the other side. Close the edge by pulling the yarn snugly enough to hide the bound-off edges and continue to the next stitch. Note that you must have the same number of stitches on each piece to be joined.

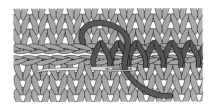

invisible vertical to horizontal for setting in sleeves

Insert the yarn needle under a stitch inside the bound-off edge of the vertical piece. Now insert the yarn needle under one or two horizontal bars (as appropriate: one bar is appropriate when the length of the vertical and horizontal piece is identical, and two bars are appropriate when easing in fullness) between the first and second stitches of the horizontal piece. Continue in this manner.

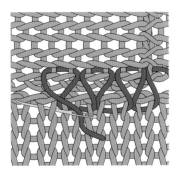

Two horizontal bars are picked up along each bound-off edge.

invisible vertical on stockinette stitch for side and underarm seams

This technique joins edges row by row, hides selvage stitches, and makes your knitting appear continuous. Insert the yarn needle under the horizontal bar between the first and second stitches. Insert the needle into the corresponding bar on the other piece. Secure seam gently yet firmly and continue alternating from side to side.

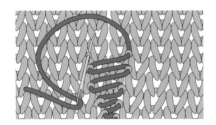

invisible vertical on reverse stockinette stitch for side and underarm seams

Instead of working into the horizontal strand between stitches, work into the stitch itself. Insert the yarn needle into the top loop of the stitch inside the edge on one side, and then in the bottom loop of the corresponding stitch on the other side. Secure the seam gently yet firmly and continue alternating side to side.

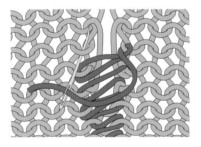

whipstitch

With threaded yarn needle, and working from right to left, make slanted stitches about 1/8" to 1/4" deep and 1/8" to 1/4" apart (depending on weight of knit fabric; closer for finer knits). Make stitches one at a time and pull the yarn through snugly without pulling the knitting too tight.

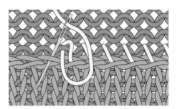

selvage stitches

The selvage stitch is an edge formed by adding one stitch at both the beginning and end of the pattern stitch(es). All patterns in this book include selvage stitches.

The selvage stitch is your seam allowance. It helps create a firm edge and will not be seen when the garment is seamed. I prefer to use K1 on both right and wrong sides for my selvage stitches, although P1 can be used for your selvage stitch should it seem more appropriate for a stitch pattern you are using. There may be times when more than one selvage stitch is appropriate: in an openwork pattern, with a slippery silk or rayon yarn, or as a decorative edge on a scarf. Generally speaking and throughout the patterns in this book, one selvage stitch per edge is sufficient and does not add bulk to the seams.

swatching

Swatching is the actual knitting of a stitch pattern you plan to use in a knit garment. Swatches are most often knit in a 4" by 4" square. Swatching is an essential part of creating the sweater you want. Not only does it confirm gauge, but it tells you if the yarn you have chosen will give you the look you want for your garment, particularly in terms of weight and drape. Pin your swatch down as if to block it when calculating gauge.

t

tea

Tea is a lovely accompaniment for sitting and knitting, and it offers us many health benefits. For example, tea has isoflavonoids, which actually increase bone density, unlike coffee, which causes calcium loss.

texture

Texture is what I am drawn to as a knitter and really what this book is about. Cables, bobbles, yarn overs, and ribbing create texture in knitting. I believe solid-colored textured knits offer an appeal that we never tire of, and they can be worn for many years.

three-needle bind off

Three-needle bind off is used in the Triple Braided Diamonds Turtleneck on page 83 and produces a lovely seam. To work, place right sides together with back stitches on one needle and front stitches on another. Using a third needle of the same size, *knit two stitches together (one from front needle and one from back needle)*, repeat from * to * once and pass first stitch over second stitch. Repeat this until all stitches are bound off, and secure edge.

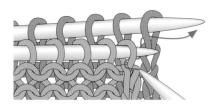

two at a time

When knitting sleeves, I always cast on stitches for both sleeves with separate balls of yarn and work them at the same time. I feel it actually saves time to only have to work out shaping once. The same is true for knitting front sides of a cardigan and neckline edges at the same time. It facilitates seeing how the reverse shaping works for the opposite side as well.

u

unraveling

Never hesitate to unravel to correct a mistake. Most yarns, but not all, can be reknit.

v

value

The value of hand-knit projects is priceless. A hand knit item is made with time and love. I like to remember that each stitch is hand knit.

w

Walker

Barbara Walker, knitter and mentor extraordinaire, had the great insight to collect stitch patterns and offer them to us in reference form in her well-known books, which are aptly named and treasures that encourage creativity in knitters. See "Bibliography" on page 96 for more information regarding these books.

x

Xcellence

"Xcellence," or excellence, is the quality we can strive for in our knitting. Look at your work often, perhaps every time you put it down and pick it up. Check for accuracy. If you see a mistake, correct it. If you check regularly, you won't have that far to go back and most likely will have a greater appreciation of the finished work.

X marks the back

Since a knit garment takes on the shape of our body, for sweaters in which the neckline is the same on both sides, mark the back with an X. I like to make a small X at the center of the back neck with double-stranded, slightly contrasting-colored sewing thread. The X makes it easy to tell which way to put the sweater on when getting dressed. Sweaters that might need this are Roman Stripe Boatneck on page 30, Mosaic Boatneck on page 38, Stripes and Web Boatneck on page 42, and Peri's Parasol Pullover on page 47.

y

yarn

Yarn is the fabric of our craft, and has there ever been a time when more beautiful yarns were available to us as knitters? Be inspired.

The way that a yarn is woven or the way that the individual fibers are put together influences the resilience of the yarn. For the designs in *The Pleasures of Knitting*, yarns in natural fibers will work well and are more appropriate choices than synthetic yarns.

Wool has memory or elasticity, which allows it to spring back to its original shape when stretched, and that is why wool sweaters tend to retain their shape better than cotton sweaters. Cotton sweaters will hold their shape better if the cotton yarn is a cable weave, mercerized, and/or an Egyptian cotton. There are a number of cotton blends available that are 80% cotton and 20% wool, which helps the cotton hold its shape. Cotton from Egypt is among the highest quality in the world because of its fine and smooth fibers. Mercerized cotton is treated so that the fibers are stretched and become smoother and stronger with a slight sheen. Cable weave means that the individual threads of yarn that make up a strand are more interlocked than in a yarn in

which the strands are simply twisted together. Also, because of the amount of texture used in many of my designs, if you make them in 100% cotton yarn, I encourage you to use a cable weave or strong twist. A yarn with a loose twist tends to split or the strands can separate as you knit; it will also be more likely to stretch out as you wear it. When shopping for yarn, play with the end of the skein a little bit to get a feeling for how tightly it is or is not twisted. You can determine this by how easily the strands separate.

yarn substitutions

The following are yarn substitution lists for the yarns used in the projects in this book.

fingering-weight substitutions

Sesia Cable 2005 may be challenging to find; see "Resources" on page 96. Appropriate alternatives include the following 100% cottons and cotton-wool blends:

- 4 Ply Cotton from Rowan, 100%
- Baby Merino 4 Ply from Jaeger, 100% merino wool
- Madelaine from Knit One Crochet Too, 100% superfine merino wool
- Mandarin Petit from Sandnes, 100% Egyptian cotton, available from Ram Wools at www.ramwools.com and Awesome Ewe at www.awesomeewe.com
- Nature Spun Fingering from Brown sheep, 100% wool
- Siena 4 Ply from Jaeger, 100% mercerized cotton
- Wool/Cotton from Debbie Bliss, 50% wool, 50% cotton

DK-weight substitutions

Tahki Cotton Classic is readily available and consistently excellent quality yarn. It is interchangeable with the following:

- Butterfly Super 10 from S. R. Kertzer, 100% mercerized cotton
- Endless Summer Collection Sonata, 100% mercerized cotton, available only from Elann at www.elann.com

heavy worsted-weight substitutions

- Fantasy Naturale from Plymouth, 100% mercerized cotton
- Sierra from Cascade Yarns, 80% pima cotton, 20% highland wool
- Willow from Tahki Yarns, 66% linen, 34% cotton

Z

completion

Z is the end of the alphabet, and in knitting the end is *completion*. Finish each project that you start and know that it is okay to have more than one work in progress.

approx	approximately		**PM**	place marker
b/B	back		**psso**	pass slip stitch(es) over
beg	beginning		**p2sso**	pass 2 slip stitches over
BO	bind off		**PU**	pick up and knit
C	cable		**pw**	purlwise
cn	cable needle		**R**	right
CO	cast on		**rem**	remaining
cont	continue		**rep**	repeat
dec(s)	decrease(s)		**rnd(s)**	round(s)
dpn	double-pointed needles		**RS**	right side
EOR	every other row		**RSR**	right side row
f/F	front		**sk**	skip
g	gram		**sl**	slip
inc(s)	increase(s)		**SSK**	slip, slip, knit: slip 1 st as if to knit, slip 1 st as if to knit, insert left needle into front of the 2 sts, knit the 2 sts tog
K	knit			
K1f&b&f	knit into front, back, and front of same stitch			
K2tog	knit 2 stitches together		**SSP**	slip, slip, purl: slip 1 st as if to knit, slip 1 st as if to knit, return the 2 sts back to left needle, purl 2 sts tog through the back loops
kw	knitwise			
L	left			
M1 kw	make 1 stitch knitwise: pick up horizontal bar between 2 stitches from back to front and knit into front of stitch			
			st(s)	stitch(es)
			St st	stockinette stitch
			tbl	through back loop(s)
M1 pw	make 1 stitch purlwise: pick up horizontal bar between 2 stitches from front to back and purl into back of stitch		**tog**	together
			wyib	with yarn in back
			wyif	with yarn in front
			WS	wrong side
MB	make bobble		**WSR**	wrong side row
P	purl		**yds**	yards
P1f&b	purl into front and back of same stich		**YO**	yarn over
P2tog	purl 2 stitches together			

Skill Levels

■□□□ Beginner

■■□□ Easy

■■■□ Intermediate

■■■■ Experienced

Standard Yarn-Weight System

Yarn-Weight Symbol & Category Names	1 SUPER FINE	2 FINE	3 LIGHT	4 MEDIUM	5 BULKY	6 SUPER BULKY
Types of Yarns in Category	Sock, Fingering, Baby	Sport, Baby	DK, Light Worsted	Worsted, Afghan, Aran	Chunky, Craft, Rug	Bulky, Roving
Knit-Gauge Ranges in Stockinette Stitch to 4"	27 to 32 sts	23 to 26 sts	21 to 24 sts	16 to 20 sts	12 to 15 sts	6 to 11 sts
Recommended Needle in US Size Range	1 to 3	3 to 5	5 to 7	7 to 9	9 to 11	11 and larger

Vertical Rib Pullover

This sweater is an updated version of the "poor boy" sweater from the mid-1960s. It has clean lines, is fitted, is slightly cropped, and has three-quarter-length sleeves. If you like the bare midriff look, then simply make the sweater an inch shorter by eliminating nine rows after you complete the ribbing for the front and before you begin the ribbing on the back. This sweater is knit in one piece and seaming is minimized by the elimination of shoulder seams and set-in sleeves.

Skill Level:

Materials

- 7 (8, 9, 10) balls of Jaeger Siena 4 Ply (100% mercerized cotton; 50 g; 153 yds), color 401 ❶
- Size 3 needles or size required to obtain gauge
- Size 3 circular needles (40")
- Size 2 needles
- Size 2 circular needles (24")
- Coilless knitter's safety pins
- Row counter

Size: Petite (Small, Medium, Large)
Finished Measurements
Bust: 33½ (35, 37½, 39)"
Length: 18 (19, 20, 21)"

Gauge

27 sts and 36 rows = 4" in patt st on size 3 needles when blocked

Pattern Stitch

Vertical Rib

Row 1 (RS): (K3, P3) across.
Row 2: (P3, K3) across.
Rep these 2 rows for patt.

Front, Sleeves, Neck Opening, and Back

Sweater is worked in 1 piece, beg at bottom front, up and over shoulders to bottom back.

- With smaller needles, cable CO 105 (111, 119, 125) sts. Work bottom ribbing as follows:
  Row 1 (RS): K1, *P1, K1, rep from *.
  Row 2: K2, *P1, K1, rep from *.
  Rows 3–12: Rep rows 1 and 2.
- Change to larger needles, establish main patt as follows:
  Row 1 (RS): K1, P2 (2, 3, 3), *K3, P3, rep from * to last 6 (6, 7, 7) sts, K3, P2 (2, 3, 3), K1.
  Row 2: K3 (3, 4, 4), *P3, K3, rep from * to last 6 (6, 7, 7) sts, P3, K3 (3, 4, 4). Rep rows 1 and 2 for a total of 20 (24, 30, 34) rows in main patt; work measures approx 3½ (4, 4½, 5)" from beg of ribbing.

Row 21 (25, 31, 35) of main patt: Inc 1 st each edge between selvage st and first st and between last st and selvage st by using M1 kw or pw as appropriate for patt. Rep inc row every 12 rows 3 times more—113 (119, 127, 133) sts; 57 (61, 67, 71) rows from beg of main patt.

- Work even for 11 rows more—68 (72, 78, 82) rows from beg of main patt.

- **Beg armhole shaping on row 69 (73, 79, 83) of main patt:** Inc 2 sts by using knit-on CO at beg of next 12 rows. CO 7 sts at beg of next 22 (30, 30, 30) rows. CO 6 sts at beg of next 8 (0, 0, 0) rows. CO 3 sts at beg of next 2 rows. CO 0 (0, 1, 3) sts at beg of next 0 (0, 2, 2) rows—345 (359, 369, 379) sts; 112 (116, 124, 128) rows from beg of main patt. When sleeve incs no longer fit easily on straight needles, change to 40" circular needles.

- Work even for 12 (18, 20, 26) rows more—124 (134, 144, 154) rows from beg of main patt; work measures approx 15½ (16½, 17½, 18½)" from beg of ribbing.

- **Beg neck shaping on row 125 (135, 145, 155) of main patt:** Work in patt across 156 (161, 165, 169) sts, attach 2nd ball of yarn and BO center 33 (37, 39, 41) sts, finish row. Work both sides at same time with 2 separate balls of yarn, at beg of each neck edge on EOR, dec 1 st, then BO 3 (4, 4, 4) sts once.

Dec 1 st, then BO 2 (2, 3, 3) sts once. Dec 1 st, then BO 0 (1, 1, 1) st once. Dec 1 st 4 times—144 (147, 150, 154) sts each side of neck.

- Work even for 11 rows more. Mark row 145 (155, 165, 175) with safety pin at neck edge and cuff to indicate center of garment or where shoulder seam would be if there were one.

- **Beg back neck shaping on row 151 (161, 171, 181) of main patt:** Work both sides at same time with 2 separate balls of yarn, at beg of each neck edge on EOR use knit-on CO to CO 6 (7, 7, 7) sts twice. CO 10 (11, 12, 13) sts once. On next row of 1 neck edge only, CO 13 (15, 17, 17) sts and join neck edges for original number of sts—345 (359, 369, 379) sts.

Tip: When joining neck edges, work first 2 or 3 sts using both attached strands to reinforce the connection before dropping to a single strand and cutting and securing the dropped strand. Remember not to confuse the double strand of yarn used for the first 2 or 3 sts for more than 1 st when you work the next row.

- Work even until cuff edge of sleeve is symmetrical on front and back.

- **Beg armhole shaping:** BO 0 (0, 1, 3) sts at beg of next 0 (0, 2, 2) rows. Dec 1 st, then BO 2 sts at beg of next 2 rows. Dec 1 (0, 0, 0) st, then BO 5 sts at beg of next 8 (0, 0, 0) rows. Dec 1 st, then BO 6 sts at beg of next 22 (30, 30, 30) rows. Dec 1 st, then BO 1 st at beg of next 12 rows—113 (119, 127, 133) sts. Work even for 11 rows more.

- **Next row:** Dec 1 st each edge by working K1 (selvage st), K2tog or P2tog as appropriate for where you are in patt, work to last 3 sts and either SSK or SSP as appropriate for where you are in patt, K1 (selvage st). Rep

dec each edge every 12 rows 3 times more—
105 (111, 119, 125) sts. Work even for 20
(24, 30, 34) rows more.

✦ Change to smaller needles and work 12 rows
in bottom ribbing. Note that first row of ribbing will be WS row, so beg P1, *K1, P1*,
rep from * to *.

Finishing

✦ **Sleeve edge:** With RS of garment facing you,
and smaller needles, PU 57 (63, 71, 77) sts
and work in ribbing as for front and back
lower edges.

✦ Block to measurements, making sure all vertical ribs are straight.

✦ Sew side seams using a combination of invisible vertical on St st seaming (page 20) and
invisible vertical on reverse St st seaming
(page 20) as appropriate in patt st. Sew
underarm seams using invisible horizontal
seaming (page 19).

✦ **Neck edge:** With WS of garment facing you,
and smaller circular needles, PU 6 sts per
inch around neck edge—approx 138 (150,
162, 168) sts. With RS of inside neck edging

facing you, knit 6 rnds, purl 1 rnd (this will
become fold line), knit 6 rnds and BO on
next rnd. The smooth side of St st is RS,
bumpy purl side will face in once you fold at
purl row and will not be seen. After folding
on purl row, pin neck edging evenly, taking
care to cover raw edges. With yarn needle
and tail, sew in and out of BO loops to
attach.

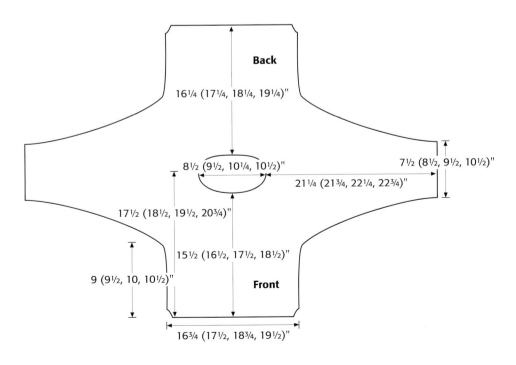

Roman Stripe Boatneck

Roman Stripe Boatneck is so easy to make and wear.

It goes very quickly and its versatility adds to

its appeal. The sleeves are three-quarter length.

Wear this sweater over a camisole in the summer

or a T-shirt in the spring and fall.

Skill Level:

Size: Petite (Small, Medium, Large, Extra Large)

Finished Measurements
Bust: 36 (38, 40, 42, 45)"
Length: 21½ (23, 23, 24½, 26)"

Materials

- 7 (8, 8, 9, 9) skeins of Tahki Cotton Classic (100% mercerized cotton; 50 g; 108 yds), color 3818 (3)
- Size 8 needles

Gauge

14 sts and 25½ rows = 4" in patt st when blocked

Pattern Stitch

Roman Stripe

Over even number of sts.
Row 1 (RS): K2, *YO, K1, rep from * to last 2 sts, K2.
Row 2: K1, purl across, end K1.
Row 3: K2, *K2tog, rep from * to last 2 sts, K2.
Rows 4 and 5: K2, *YO, K2tog, rep from * to last 2 sts, K2.
Rows 6, 7, and 8: Knit.
Rep these 8 rows for patt.

Front and Back

- With size 8 needles, cable CO 64 (68, 72, 76, 80) sts and work first 4 rows as follows:
  Rows 1 and 3 (RS): K1 (selvage st), purl across row to last st, end K1.
  Rows 2 and 4: Knit.
- Beg Roman stripe patt st and cont until work measures 14 (15, 15, 16, 17)" from beg, ending with completed patt row 6.
- Armhole shaping:
  Patt row 7: BO kw 3 sts at beg of row, knit rem sts.
  Patt row 8: BO pw 3 sts at beg of row, knit rem sts.
  Dec 2 sts at beg of next 2 rows as follows:
  Patt row 1: K2tog, K1, pass K2tog over K1, K1, *YO, K1, rep from * to last 3 sts, K3.
  Patt row 2: P2tog, P1, pass P2tog over P1, purl to end of row.
  Dec 1 st at beg of next 2 rows as follows:
  Patt row 3: *K2tog, rep from * to last st, end K1.
  Patt row 4: K2tog, K1, *YO, K2tog, rep from * to last 2 sts, K2.
- Cont in patt on rem 52 (56, 60, 64, 68) sts until armhole measures 7 (7½, 7½, 8, 8½)".
- Work last 4 rows same as rows 1–4 at beg.
- **Next row:** BO kw all sts.

Sleeves

- Cable CO 36 sts. Work first 4 rows as for front and back, except on row 4 inc 1 st each edge by using M1 kw after beg selvage st and before last selvage st—38 sts.

- Beg Roman stripe patt st and work 86 rows, working incs at each edge by using M1 kw after first st and before last st, beg on row 7 (3, 3, 3, 7) and working inc every 12 (10, 10, 8, 6) rows a total of 7 (9, 9, 11, 13) times—52 (56, 56, 60, 64) sts. Note that when working inc on patt row 3, it will be K1, M1 kw, K1, *K2tog, rep from * to last 2 sts, K1, M1 kw, K1.

- Shape cap:

  Patt row 7: BO kw 3 sts at beg of row, knit rem sts.

  Patt row 8: BO pw 3 sts at beg of row, knit rem sts.

Dec 2 sts at beg of next 2 rows as follows:

Patt row 1: K2tog, K1, pass K2tog over K1, K1, *YO, K1, rep from * to last 3 sts, K3.

Patt row 2: P2tog, P1, pass P2tog over P1, purl rem sts, end K1.

Dec 1 st at beg of next 16 rows as follows:

Patt row 3: *K2tog, rep from * to last st, end K1.

Patt row 4: K2tog, K1, *YO, K2tog, rep from * to last 3 sts, K3.

Patt row 5: K2tog, *YO, K2tog, rep from * to last 2 sts, K2.

Patt row 6: P2tog, knit rem sts.

Patt row 7: K2tog, knit rem sts.

Patt row 8: P2tog, knit rem sts.

Patt row 1: K2tog, K1, *YO, K1, rep from * to last 3 sts, K3.

Patt row 2: P2tog, purl rem sts.

Patt row 3: *K2tog, rep from * to last 2 sts, end K2.

Patt row 4: P2tog, K1, *YO, K2tog, rep from * to last 2 sts, K2.

Patt row 5: K2tog, K2, *YO, K2tog, rep from * to last 2 sts, K2.

Patt row 6: P2tog, knit rem sts.

Patt row 7: K2tog, knit rem sts.

Patt row 8: P2tog, knit rem sts.

Patt row 1: K2tog, K1, *YO, K1, rep from * to last 3 sts, K3.

Patt row 2: P2tog, purl rem sts.

Dec 2 sts at beg of next 6 rows as follows:

Patt row 3: K2tog, K2tog and pass first K2tog over second K2tog, *K2tog, rep from * to last 2 sts, end K2.

Patt row 4: P2tog, P1, pass P2tog over P1, *YO, K2tog, rep from * to last 3 sts, K3.

Patt row 5: K2tog, K1, pass K2tog over K1, K2, *YO, K2tog, rep from * to last 3 sts, K3.

Patt row 6: P2tog, P1, pass P2tog over P1, knit rem sts.

Patt row 7: K2tog, K1, pass K2tog over K1, knit rem sts.

Patt row 8: P2tog, P1, pass P2tog over P1, knit rem sts.

+ Purl 1 row (RS), knit 1 row, purl 1 row, and BO kw rem 14 (18, 18, 22, 26) sts.

Finishing

+ Block all pieces, really opening up sts and stretching out work to measurements.
+ Sew shoulder seams 1½ (1¾, 2, 2½, 3)" for each shoulder using invisible horizontal seaming (page 19).
+ Sew side and underarm seams using invisible vertical on St st seaming (page 20) and reverse St st seaming (page 20) as appropriate.

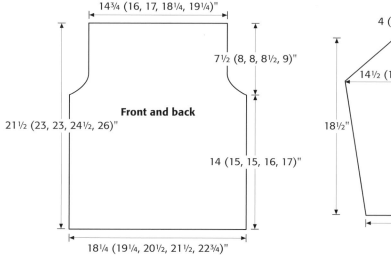

14¾ (16, 17, 18¼, 19¼)"

7½ (8, 8, 8½, 9)"

Front and back

21½ (23, 23, 24½, 26)"

14 (15, 15, 16, 17)"

18¼ (19¼, 20½, 21½, 22¾)"

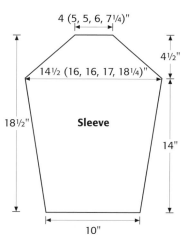

4 (5, 5, 6, 7¼)"

4½"

14½ (16, 16, 17, 18¼)"

18½"

Sleeve

14"

10"

Summer Stripe Cap-Sleeve Shell

Easy to knit and easy to wear,

Summer Stripe Cap-Sleeve Shell is flattering,

versatile, and cool on a summer day.

It's also very lovely with a shawl

thrown around the shoulders.

Skill Level:

■■□□

Materials

- 5 (5, 6, 6) skeins of Tahki Cotton Classic (100% mercerized cotton; 50 g; 108 yds), color 3002, Black
- Size 8 needles *or* size required to obtain gauge
- Size 7 needles
- Size 7 circular needles (16")
- 2 small black buttons and small-gauge round elastic in black, or 2 hooks and eyes

Gauge

18 sts and 25 rows = 4" on size 8 needles when blocked

Size: Petite (Small, Medium, Large)

Finished Measurements
Bust: 36½ (38, 40, 41½)"
Length: 19¾ (20¼, 20¾, 21¼)"

Back

- With smaller needles, cable CO 82 (86, 90, 94) sts. Work 5 rows in garter st with 1 selvage st at each edge.
- Change to larger needles.
  Row 6 (RS): K1 *YO, P2tog, rep from * to last st, K1.
  Rows 7–9: Knit.
  Rows 10–17: Rep rows 6–9 twice.
  Rows 18–26: Work 9 rows in St st.
  Rows 27 and 29: Knit.
  Row 28: Rep row 6.
  Rep rows 18–29 until a total of 83 rows have been worked from beg and work measures approx 13¼".

- Shape armhole: BO 3 sts at beg of next 2 rows. Dec 1 st, BO 1 st at beg of next 2 rows—72 (76, 80, 84) sts. Work in patt as established until armhole measures 6 (6½, 7, 7½)".

- Shape neck and shoulder: Work in patt across 29 (31, 33, 35) sts, join a second ball of yarn and BO center 14 sts, finish row. Work both sides at same time. *With 1 ball of yarn, BO 6 (7, 8, 8) sts at shoulder edge, and with other ball of yarn dec 1 st, then BO 4 sts at neck edge of same row*, rep from * to * on next row. Cont in this manner with 2 balls of yarn. On next 2 rows, dec 1 st, then BO 5 (6, 7, 8) at shoulder edge, and dec 1 st, then BO 3 sts at neck edge of same row. Dec 1 st, then BO 7 (7, 7, 8) sts at shoulder edge on next 2 rows.

Front

- Work as for back until piece measures 17½ (18, 18½, 19)".
- **Shape neck:** Work in patt across 29 (31, 33, 35) sts, join a 2nd ball of yarn and BO center 14 sts, finish row. Cont with 2 balls of yarn, at beg of each neck edge on EOR. Dec 1 st, then BO 3 sts once. Dec 1 st and BO 1 st once. Dec 1 st once. Dec 1 st once AND AT SAME TIME, beg shoulder shaping as for back.

Finishing

- Block pieces to measurements, opening up the stitches as you pin for blocking.
- Sew shoulder seams using invisible horizontal seaming (page 19).
- Sew side seams using invisible vertical on St st seaming (page 20).

- **Mock Turtleneck:** With smaller circular needles, PU 68 sts starting at center back of neckline. Work in the rnd as follows:

  Rnds 1 and 3 (RS): Purl.

  Rnds 2 and 4: Knit.

  Row 5: Beg back of neck opening (turn so work is no longer in the rnd): K1, P2tog, *YO, P2tog*, rep from * to *, end P2tog, K1.

  Rows 6, 7, and 8: K2, purl across, end K2.

  Rows 9–20: Rep rows 5–8 another 3 times and bind off rem 60 sts on last row 8.

- **Arm Edging:** With smaller circular needles, PU 56 (60, 64, 68) sts along armhole edge. Work in the rnd as follows:

  Rnd 1 and 2: Purl all sts.

  Next rnd: BO kw all sts.

  Rep for 2nd armhole edge.

- At back of neck placket, sew 2 small buttons in place. Sew black round elastic in loop to other edge for button closure, or sew on 2 small hooks and eyes for closure.

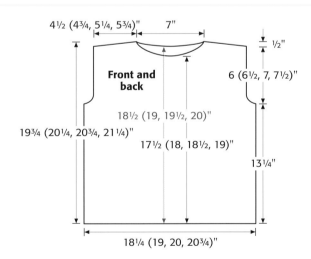

4½ (4¾, 5¼, 5¾)"   7"

½"

Front and back

6 (6½, 7, 7½)"

19¾ (20¼, 20¾, 21¼)"

18½ (19, 19½, 20)"

17½ (18, 18½, 19)"

13¼"

18¼ (19, 20, 20¾)"

Mosaic Boatneck

Mosaic Boatneck is an oversized, longer length pullover sweater with a rolled-edge boatneck.

It is subtle and simple as well as comfortable and cozy: a sweater you can curl up in.

Each piece is knit from top to bottom rather than the usual bottom to top.

Sleeves are bracelet length.

Skill Level:

Materials

- 18 (23) balls of Bernat Handicrafter Cotton (100% cotton; 50g; 80 yds), color Baby Pink **(4)**
- 1 spool of heavy-duty thread or quilting thread in 100% cotton to match yarn color
- Size 8 needles or size required to obtain gauge
- Size 6 needles

Gauge

18 sts and 28 rows = 4" in patt st on size 8 needles blocked

Size: Small/Medium (Large/Extra Large)

Finished Measurements
Bust: 40 (48)"
Length: 24½"

Pattern Stitch

Pavilion

Multiple of 18 sts

Row 1 (RS): *K2, P1, K5, P7, K3, rep from *.

Row 2 and all WS rows: Knit all knit sts and purl all purl sts.

Row 3: *(K1, P1) twice, K5, P5, K4, rep from *.

Row 5: P1, K3, P1, K5, P3, K5, rep from *.

Row 7: *K5, P1, K5, P7, rep from *.

Row 9: *(P1, K5) twice, P5, K1, rep from *.

Row 11: *K1, (P1, K5) twice, P3, K2, rep from *.

Row 13: K2, *P1, K5, rep from *, end last rep with K3.

Row 15: *K3, P1, K5, P1, K3, P1, K1, P1, K2, rep from *.

Row 17: *K4, P1, K5, P1, K1, P1, K3, P1, K1, rep from *.

Row 19: *K5, P7, K5, P1, rep from *.

Row 21: *P1, K5, P5, K5, P1, K1, rep from *.

Row 23: *K1, P1, K5, P3, K5, P1, K2, rep from *.

Row 25: *K2, P7, K5, P1, K3, rep from *.

Row 27: *K1, P1, K1, P5, K5, P1, K4, rep from *.

Row 29: * P1, K3, P3, K5, P1, K5, rep from *.

Row 31: *K5, P1, rep from *.

Row 33: *K4, P1, K1, P1, K3, P1, K5, P1, K1, rep from *.

Row 35: *(K3, P1) twice, K1, P1, K5, P1, K2, rep from *.

Row 36: Rep row 2.

Rep these 36 rows for patt.

Back and Front

Back and front are worked from shoulder down.

- With smaller needles, cable CO 90 (108) sts with 1 strand each of yarn and cotton thread held tog (so work holds its shape) and work 16 rows in St st.
- Change to larger needles, working with yarn only, work rows 1–36 of pavilion patt st a total of 4 times—144 rows in pavilion patt; total 160 rows from beg.
- Change to smaller needles. Add 1 strand of cotton thread to yarn. On RS row, knit 1 row and dec 9 sts evenly spaced across row—81 (99) sts.
- Work 9 rows in K1, P1 ribbing and on next row BO in patt.

Sleeves

Sleeves are worked from shoulder down.

- With smaller needles, cable CO 98 (104) sts with 1 strand each of yarn and cotton thread held tog, and work 16 rows in St st, working 1 dec at each edge every 4 rows 4 times—90 (96) sts.
- Change to larger needles and working with yarn only, beg pavilion patt st. Note that size L/XL will have an extra K2 at beg and end of row. Work in patt, dec as follows:

Dec 1 st each edge every 3 rows 12 times— 66 (72) sts.

Dec 1 st each edge every 4 rows 9 times—48 (54) sts.

Dec 1 st each edge every 5 rows 3 times—42 (48) sts.

Work through row 18 (24) of pavilion patt for total of 16 (17)".

- Change to smaller needles. Add 1 strand of cotton thread to yarn. On RS row, knit 1 row and dec 8 sts evenly spaced across row—34 (40) sts.
- Work 9 rows in K1, P1 ribbing and on next row BO in patt.

Finishing

- Block pieces to measurements.
- Sew shoulder seams with WS tog using a backstitch.
- Sew sleeves to front and back with WS tog using a backstitch.
- Sew side seams and underarm seams with RS facing out, using invisible vertical on St st seaming (page 20).

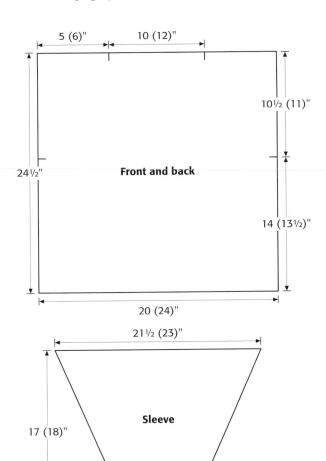

Backstitch

The shoulders and sleeves of this garment are sewn with WS together using a backstitch.

1. Thread a needle with yarn. Working in the 2nd row below the bind off, secure the beginning of the seam by bringing the yarn around the seam edges twice. Then bring the needle back up approximately ¼" from where the yarn last emerged.

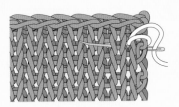

2. Insert the needle into the point where the yarn emerged from the previous stitch and bring it back up approx ¼" to the left. Pull the yarn through. Repeat for entire seam, keeping stitches even so that the finished seam will not pucker or distort.

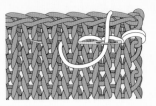

Stripes and Web Boatneck

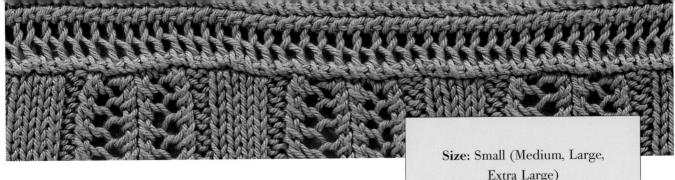

Light and airy without being too sheer,

Stripes and Web Boatneck offers a classic silhouette

with a contemporary stitch approach.

The beaded rib pattern adds another

interesting textural element.

Skill Level:

Materials

+ 10 (11, 12, 13) balls of Rowan Cotton Glace (100% cotton; 50 g; 125 yds), color 749, Sky **2**
+ Size 3 needles or size required to obtain gauge
+ Size 3 circular needles (24")
+ Size 1 needles
+ Size 1 circular needles (24")

Gauge

24 sts and 30 rows = 4" in vertical web st on size 3 needles when blocked

Size: Small (Medium, Large, Extra Large)

Finished Measurements
Bust: 34½ (37, 40, 42½)"
Length: 19½ (20½, 21½, 22½)"

Pattern Stitches

Beaded Rib

Multiple of 5 sts
Worked in the rnd.
Rnd 1 (RS): *P2, K1, P1, K1, rep from *.
Rnd 2: *P2, K3, rep from *.
Rep these 2 rnds for patt.

Worked back and forth.
Row 1 (RS): *P2, K1, P1, K1, rep from * to last 2 sts, P2.
Row 2: *K2, P3, rep from * to last 2 sts, K2.
Rep these 2 rows for patt.

Vertical Web

Multiple of 4 sts
Worked back and forth.
Row 1 (RS): *K2, YO, sl 1, K1, psso, rep from *.
Row 2: *P2, YO, P2tog, rep from *.
Rep these 2 rows for patt, except when working in the rnd, rnd 2 will be K2, YO, K2tog.

Front and Back

- With smaller circular needles, cable CO 170 (185, 200, 215) sts. Join and work in beaded rib patt, PM at beg of rnd to mark side seam, and PM halfway around to mark other side seam. Cont in patt for 3", end with completed RS row.

- Change to larger circular needles. **Next rnd:** Knit around and use M1 kw to inc 38 (39, 40, 41) sts evenly spaced—208 (224, 240, 256) sts. Establish vertical web patt as follows:

  Rnd 1: *K4, P2, (K2, YO, sl 1, K1, psso) twice, P2*, rep from * to * to beg of rnd marker.

Rnd 2: *K4, P2, (K2, YO, K2tog) 2 times, P2*, rep from * to * to beg of rnd marker.

Rep rnds 1 and 2 until work measures 12 (12½, 13, 13½)" from beg or desired length to underarm, end at first marker. Work to second marker in patt, turn. Sl rem 104 (112, 120, 128) sts to holder to work later for back.

- Change to larger straight needles, work back and forth in vertical web patt, and shape armholes: BO 3 sts at beg of next 2 rows, dec 1 st at beg of next 10 rows—88 (96, 104, 112) sts. Work even until armhole measures approx 3½ (4, 4½, 5)", BO all sts.

- Sl sts for back to larger straight needles and work as for front.

Sleeves and Yoke

- **First sleeve:** With smaller needles, cable CO 52 (62, 72, 82) sts and work rows 1 and 2 of beaded ribbing back and forth for a total of 14 rows.

- Change to larger needles, work rows 1 and 2 of vertical web st as follows:

  Row 1 (RS): *K4, P2, (K2, YO, sl 1, K1, psso) twice, P2*, rep from * to *, end each size as follows:

  For Small, end K4.

  For Medium, end K4, P2, (K2, YO, sl 1, K1, psso) twice.

  For Large, end K4, P2, K2.

  For Extra Large, end K2.

  Row 2 (WS): *P4, K2, (P2, YO, P2tog) twice, K2*; rep from * to *, end each size as follows:

  For Small, end P4.

  For Medium, end P4, K2, (P2, YO, P2tog) twice.

  For Large, end P4, K2, P4.

  For Extra Large, end P2.

  Rep these 2 rows, inc 1 st each edge beg row 7 (8, 8, 8) and cont to work inc every 7 (8, 8, 12) rows 15 (14, 14, 10) times—84 (92, 102, 104) sts. Note that you should work incs in patt as number of inc sts allows you to do so. Work 114 (118, 122, 126) rows; piece will measure approx 16½ (17, 17½, 18)". Or work to desired length from beg of sleeve.

- **Shape cap:** BO 6 sts at beg of next 2 rows, dec 1 st each edge every row until 44 sts rem. Work even in patt until work measures 5¼ (5¾, 6¾, 7¾)" from beg of cap shaping, ending with completed WS row.

- **Neck opening and front yoke: Next row (RS):** Work in patt across first 22 sts and place rem 22 sts on holder for back yoke.

  Row 1 (WS): Beg at neck edge, inc 1 in first st by knitting in front and back of st, work in seed st across next 5 sts, cont in established patt, end P1 (selvage st).

  Row 2: Work in patt as established over first 16 sts and work rem sts in seed st.

  Rep these 2 rows, inc 1 st at neck edge EOR 4 more times—27 sts. Note that last 5 seed sts at neck opening will be folded inward to create the neck facing, rem 6 seed sts will face toward RS. Work in patt for approx 4¾ (5, 5¼, 5½)" from beg of neck shaping. Mark this row for center front of neck. Work second half of neck to correspond to first half and reverse facing shaping by dec instead of inc, end with completed WS row. Place sts on holder.

- **Back yoke:** Work to correspond to front yoke and end with a WS row. Sl sts for front yoke to needle and work other shoulder to correspond to first shoulder. Mark center of last row for shoulder edge.

- **Second sleeve:** Work to correspond to first sleeve, reversing cap shaping by inc instead of dec until there are 72 (80, 90, 92) sts. Use knit CO to CO 6 sts at beg of next 2 rows—84 (92, 102, 104) sts. Cont as for first sleeve by dec instead of inc until 52 (62, 72, 82) sts rem and sleeve measures same length as first sleeve above ribbing. Change to smaller needles, work in beaded ribbing for 13 rows, and on next row BO sts in patt.

Finishing

- Block pieces to measurements.
- Sew sleeve caps to front and back armholes using invisible vertical to horizontal seaming (page 19).

- Sew front and back of yoke to bound-off edges of front and back, easing in any fullness on yoke evenly using invisible vertical to horizontal seaming (page 19).
- Sew sleeve seams using invisible vertical seaming (page 19).
- Turn neck facing to inside of garment and sew in place to WS using whipstitch (page 20).

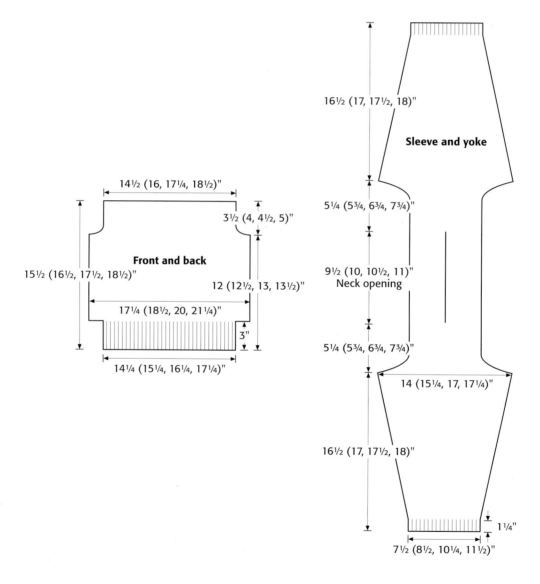

14½ (16, 17¼, 18½)"

3½ (4, 4½, 5)"

Front and back

15½ (16½, 17½, 18½)"

12 (12½, 13, 13½)"

17¼ (18½, 20, 21¼)"

3"

14¼ (15¼, 16¼, 17¼)"

16½ (17, 17½, 18)"

Sleeve and yoke

5¼ (5¾, 6¾, 7¾)"

9½ (10, 10½, 11)"
Neck opening

5¼ (5¾, 6¾, 7¾)"

14 (15¼, 17, 17¼)"

16½ (17, 17½, 18)"

1¼"

7½ (8½, 10¼, 11½)"

Size: Petite/Small (Medium/Large)

Finished Measurements
Bust: 34 (38)"
Length: 20 (22)"

Peri's Parasol Pullover is named for the charming border-pattern stitch that bears the same name. According to Barbara Walker, a well-known knitting author, this stitch is of ancient lineage. This pullover uses her modern adaptation, which is very close to the original. This sweater is reminiscent of something that actress Audrey Hepburn might have worn with her Capri pants and slipper-style shoes.

Skill Level:

Note: *For the size Small individuals who wear the Petite/Small or the size Large individuals who wear the Medium/Large, remember that the body of the sweater is knit in ribbing, which will give slightly at the bustline.*

Materials

- 8 (10) skeins of Tahki Cotton Classic (100% mercerized cotton; 50 g; 108 yds), color 3002 (3)
- Size 6 needles or size required to obtain gauge
- Size 5 circular needles (36")
- Size 5 dpn

Gauge

21.5 sts and 28 rows = 4" in patt st on larger needles when blocked

Pattern Stitch

Peri's Parasol

Multiple of 22 sts plus 1. (St count varies from row to row.)

Cluster = sl the given number of sts wyib, pass yarn to front, sl the same number of sts back to left-hand needle, pass yarn to back, sl the same sts again wyib.

Row 1 (RS): K1, *YO, (K1 tbl, P3) 5 times, K1 tbl, YO, K1, rep from *.

Row 2: P3, *(K3, P1) 4 times, K3, P5, rep from * to *, end last rep with P3.

Row 3: K1, *YO, K1 tbl, YO, (K1 tbl, P3) 5 times, (K1 tbl, YO) twice, K1, rep from *.

Row 4: P5, *(K3, P1) 4 times, K3, P9, rep from *, end last rep with P5.

Row 5: K1, *YO, K1 tbl, YO, SSK, YO, (K1 tbl, P2tog, P1) 5 times, K1 tbl, YO, K2tog, YO, K1 tbl, YO, K1, rep from *.

Row 6: P7, *(K2, P1) 4 times, K2, P13, rep from *, end last rep with P7.

Row 7: K1, *K1 tbl, (YO, SSK) twice, YO, (K1 tbl, P2) 5 times, K1 tbl, YO, (K2tog, YO) twice, K1 tbl, K1, rep from *.

Row 8: P8, *(K2, P1) 4 times, K2, P15, rep from *, end last rep with P8.

Front and Back

+ With larger needles, cable CO 91 (113) sts. Work Peri's parasol patt, including selvage sts as follows:

  Row 1 (RS): P1 (selvage st), work patt row 1, rep from * to * a total of 4 (5) times, P1 (selvage st).

  Row 2: K1, work patt row 2, rep from * to * a total of 4 (5) times, K1.

  Cont in established patt, working rows 1–14 of Peri's parasol patt a total of 4 times.

+ **Change to ribbing: Size M/L only:** Dec 10 sts evenly spaced across row 1 by using P2tog.

  Row 1 (RS): K1, P2, *K1, P3*, rep from * to *, end K1, P2, K1—91 (103) sts.

  Row 2: K3, *P1, K3*, rep from * to *, end P1, K3.

  Rep these 2 rows until work measures 12 (13)" from beg.

+ **Shape armholes:** BO 3 (4) sts at beg of next 2 rows. Dec 1 st, then BO 1 (2) sts at beg of next 2 rows—81 (91) sts. Work even to armhole depth of 6¾ (7¾)".

+ **Shape neck:** Work 19 (22) sts, attach second ball of yarn and BO center 43 (47) sts, finish row. Working both sides at same time with 2 separate balls of yarn, at beg of each neck edge on EOR, dec 1 st, then BO 2 (3) sts once. Dec 1 st, then BO 1 st once. Work 3 rows even.

Row 9: K2, *(YO, K2tog) twice, YO, K1 tbl, YO, (K1 tbl, P2tog) 5 times, (K1 tbl, YO) twice, (SSK, YO) twice, K3, rep from *, end last rep K2.

Rows 10 and 12: P10, *(K1, P1) 4 times, K1, P19, rep from *, end last rep with P10.

Row 11: SSK, *(YO, K2tog) 3 times, K1 tbl, YO, (K1 tbl, P1) 5 times, K1 tbl, YO, K1 tbl, (SSK, YO) 3 times, sl 2, K1, p2sso, rep from *, end last rep with K2tog instead of sl 2, K1, p2sso.

Row 13: K1, *(K2tog, YO) twice, K2tog, K1, K1 tbl, YO, (SSK) twice, sl 1, K2tog, psso, (K2tog) twice, YO, K1 tbl, K1, SSK, (YO, SSK) twice, K1, rep from *.

Row 14: Cluster 2, *P7, cluster 5, P7, cluster 3, rep from *, end last rep with cluster 2 instead of cluster 3.

- Shape shoulders: BO rem 14 (16) sts for each shoulder.

Sleeves

- With larger needles, cable CO 49 sts. Work rows 1–14 of Peri's parasol patt 1 time, working the rows as for back and front, except only rep from * to * in patt rows 2 times.
- Change to ribbing as for front and back, on row 5 (3) of ribbing inc 1 st each edge inside of selvage st by using M1 kw or M1 pw as appropriate. Work incs every 8 (5) rows to a total of 65 (77) sts and 70 (77) rows, 12 (13)" from beg of sleeve edge.
- Shape cap: BO 3 (4) sts at beg of next 2 rows. Dec 1 st, then BO 1 (2) st(s) at beg of next 2 rows. Dec 1 st at beg of next 16 (24) rows.

Dec 1 st, then BO 1 st at beg of next 4 rows. Dec 1 st, then BO 2 sts at beg of next 2 rows. BO rem 25 sts.

Finishing

- Meticulously block to measurements.
- Sew shoulder seams using invisible horizontal seaming (page 19).
- Sew sleeves into armholes using invisible vertical to horizontal seaming (page 19).
- Sew side seams and arm seams using invisible vertical on reverse St st seaming (page 20).
- Neck edging: With smaller circular needles, and beg at shoulder seam, PU sts evenly in gauge around neck edge. With smaller dpn, CO 2 sts, work I-cord (page 16) around neck, BO, and join edges.

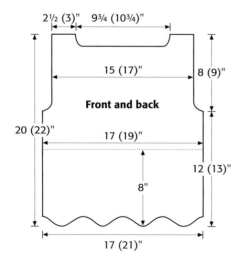

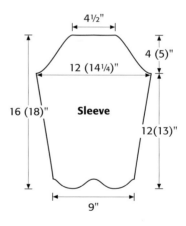

The luxury, convenience, and versatility

of a twin set are indisputable. This open, softly

sculpted version with its scalloped edges

is perfect for warm days and cool evenings.

Sleeves are bracelet length for the cardigan,

which is also great when worn with

a contrasting color underneath or over a dress.

Skill Level:

Size: Small (Medium, Large,
Extra Large)

Finished Measurements
Cardigan Bust: 34 (36, 38, 40)"
Shell Bust: 31 (33, 35, 37)"
Cardigan Length: 20½, (21½, 22½ 23½)"
Shell Length: 19 (20, 21, 22)"

Materials

+ 17 (19, 21, 23) skeins of Rowan Cotton
  Glace (100% mercerized cotton; 50g; 125
  yds), color 810, Splendour ②
+ Size 4 needles or size required to obtain
  gauge
+ Size 2 circular needles (20")
+ Size 2 circular needles (40")

Gauge

Cardigan

26 sts and 32 rows = 4" in ripple st on size 4 needles when blocked

Shell

24 sts and 32 rows = 4" in St st on size 4 needles when blocked

Pattern Stitch

Ripple

Multiple of 18 sts

Row 1 (RS): *K2tog 3 times, (K1, YO) 6 times, K2tog 3 times, rep from *.

Rows 2 and 3: Knit.

Row 4: Purl.

Rep these 4 rows for patt.

Cardigan Back

+ With larger needles, cable CO 110 (116, 122, 128) sts. Knit 2 rows. Set up ripple st patt as follows:

Row 1 (RS): K1 (selvage st), K0 (3, 6, 0), *K2tog 3 times, (K1, YO) 6 times, K2tog 3 times, rep from * to last 1 (4, 7, 1) st(s), K0 (3, 6, 0), K1 (selvage st).

Work rows 1–4 of ripple st patt a total of 25 (26, 27, 28) times—102 (106, 110, 114) rows, and approx 13 (13½, 14, 14½)" from beg.

+ **Shape armholes:** Work each size as follows:

Small

First dec row: BO kw 6 sts, work in patt as established to last 7 sts, K7.

Second dec row: BO pw 6 sts, knit to end of row—104 sts.

Third dec row: Dec 1 st, then BO 2 sts, knit to end of row.

Fourth dec row: Dec 1 st, then BO 2 sts, purl to last st, K1—98 sts.

Fifth dec row: Dec 1 st, then BO 1 st, (K1, YO) 4 times, K2tog 3 times, *K2tog 3 times, (K1, YO) 6 times, K2tog 3 times, rep from * to last 13 sts, K2tog 3 times, (K1, YO) 4 times, K3.

Sixth dec row: Dec 1 st, then BO 1 st, knit to end of row—96 sts.

Seventh dec row: Dec 1 st, knit to end of row.

Eighth dec row: Dec 1 st, purl to last st, K1—94 sts.

Main patt row 1 after working all decs is K2, (K1, YO) 3 times, K2tog 3 times, *K2tog 3 times, (K1, YO) 6 times, K2tog 3 times, rep from * to last 11 sts, K2tog 3 times, (K1, YO) 3 times, K2.

Medium

First dec row: BO kw 6 sts, K1, K2tog, (K1, YO) 6 times, *K2tog 3 times, (K1, YO) 6 times, K2tog 3 times, rep from * to last 10 sts, K2tog, K8.

Second dec row: BO pw 6 sts, knit to end of row—108 sts.

Next 2 dec rows: Dec 1 st, then BO 1 st, work in patt to end of row—104 sts after second of these 2 rows.

Main patt row 1 after decs is K1, K2tog twice, (K1, YO) 5 times, K2tog 3 times, *K2tog 3 times, (K1, YO) 6 times, K2tog 3 times, rep from * to last 16 sts, K2tog 3 times, (K1, YO) 5 times, K2tog twice, K1—104 sts.

Large

First dec row: BO kw 5 sts, work as established to last 7 sts, K7.

Second dec row: BO pw 5 sts, knit to end of row—112 sts.

Next 2 dec rows: Dec 1 st, then BO 1 st, work in patt to end of row—108 sts after second of these 2 rows.

Main patt row 1 after decs is K2, K2tog 3 times, (K1, YO) 5 times, K2tog 3 times, *K2tog 3 times, (K1, YO) 6 times, K2tog 3 times, rep from * to last 13 sts, (K1, YO) 5 times, K2tog 3 times, K2—108 sts.

Extra Large

First 2 dec rows: Work as for Small—122 sts after second of these 2 rows.

Next 2 dec rows: Work as for Small—116 sts after second of these 2 rows.

Next 2 dec rows: Work as for Small—114 sts after second of these 2 rows.

Next 2 dec rows: Work as for Small—112 sts after second of these 2 rows.

Main patt row 1 for Extra Large is same as for Small—112 sts.

Cont in established patt for all sizes until armhole depth measures 7 (7½, 8, 8½)".

Shape shoulders: Beg on patt row 1, BO 8 (9, 9, 9) sts at beg of next 2 rows; on first of these rows, BO kw, work to last 11 sts, end K11; on second of these rows, BO pw, work to last 8 (9, 9, 9) sts and purl these. Dec 1 st, BO 7 (8, 8, 8) sts at beg of next 2 rows. Dec 1 st, then BO 9 (10, 10, 10) sts at beg of next 2 rows; break patt on these 2 rows and knit entire first row, and purl entire second row. Place rem 42 (46, 50, 54) sts at back neck on holder.

Cardigan Front (Left and Right)

With larger needles, and 2 separate balls of yarn, cable CO 56 (59, 62, 65) sts for each side of front and knit 2 rows. Beg ripple st patt and establish patt for left and right fronts on patt row 1 as follows:

Left front (RS): K1 (selvage st), K0 (3, 6, 9), *K2tog 3 times, (K1, YO) 6 times, K2tog 3 times, rep from * to last st, K1 (selvage st).

Right front (RS): K1 (selvage st), *K2tog 3 times, (YO, K1) 6 times, K2tog 3 times, rep from * to last 1 (4, 7, 10) sts, K0 (3, 6, 9), K1 (selvage st).

Rep rows 1–4 in patt as established for left and right fronts a total of 23 (24, 25, 26) times—94 (98, 102, 106) rows total from beg.

✦ Shape neck: Dec 1 st at each neck edge EOR 8 times, working dec as follows:

First dec (patt row 1):

Right front, dec 1 st by omitting first YO.

Left front, dec 1 st by omitting last YO.

Second dec (patt row 3):

Right front, K4, SSK, cont in patt.

Left front, knit to last 6 sts, K2tog, K4.

Third dec (patt row 1):

Right front, K3, K2tog 2 times, (YO, K1) 4 times, cont in patt.

Left front, work in patt to last 11 sts, (K1, YO) 4 times, K2tog 2 times, K3.

Fourth dec (patt row 3): Rep second dec above.

Fifth dec (patt row 1): Dec at neck edges and AT SAME TIME beg armhole shaping:

Right front, K4, K2tog, (YO, K1) 3 times, cont in patt and for all sizes end row with K7.

Left front, BO kw 6 sts at armhole edge, cont in patt to last 9 sts, (K1, YO) 3 times, K2tog, K4.

Patt row 2: Right front, BO pw 6 sts at armhole edge, cont in patt.

Sixth dec (patt row 3): Rep second dec above at neck edges.

Left front, dec 1 st, then BO kw 2 sts at armhole edge, cont in patt.

Patt row 4: Right front, dec 1 st, then BO pw 2 sts at armhole edge, cont in patt.

Seventh dec (patt row 1):

Right front, K3, K2tog, (YO, K1) 2 times, cont in patt.

Left front, K2tog, YO, K1, YO, K1, YO, cont in patt to last 7 sts, (K1, YO) 2 times, K2tog, K3.

Patt row 2: Right front, dec 1 st, then BO pw 1 st at armhole edge, cont in patt.

Eighth dec (patt row 3):

Left front, K2tog tbl at armhole edge, knit to last 5 sts, K2tog, K3.

Patt row 4: Right front, P2tog tbl at armhole edge, purl to last 5 sts, P2tog, P3—36 (39, 42, 45) sts.

Remember all RS rows at neck edge have K3, cont in main patt as established as long as possible.

✦ Dec 1 st at each neck edge every 4 rows 4 times (on patt row 3), by working original second dec above.

- Dec 1 st at each neck edge every 6 rows 6 times as follows:

  First dec (patt row 1): Omit YO between K3 and first K2tog on right front and reverse for left front.

  Second, fourth, and sixth dec (patt row 3): Work as original second row dec above.

  Third dec (patt row 1): K1, K2tog 3 times for right front, cont in patt to end of row, and reverse for left front.

  Fifth dec (patt row 1): K1, K2tog 2 times, K1, (YO, K1) 5 times for right front, cont in patt to end of row, and reverse for left front.

- Shape shoulders as for back when armhole depth matches back.

Cardigan Sleeves

- With larger needles, cable CO 44 (48, 50, 54) sts and knit 2 rows. Work ripple st patt as follows:

  Row 1: K1 (selvage st), K2tog 1 (1, 2, 2) times, (K1, YO) 4 (5, 5, 6) times, K2tog 6 times, (K1, YO) 6 times, K2tog 6 times, (K1, YO) 4 (5, 5, 6) times, K2tog 1 (1, 2, 2) times, K1 (selvage st).

- Shape sleeve: Cont in patt, beg incs at each edge starting on row 9 (9, 13, 13) by using M1 kw between selvage st and K2tog as follows:

  Row 9 (9, 13, 13): K1, M1 kw, *K2tog 1 (1, 2, 2) times, (K1, YO) 4 (5, 5, 6) times, K2tog 6 times, (K1, YO) 6 times, K2tog 6 times, (K1, YO) 4 (5, 5, 6) times, K2tog 1 (1, 2, 2) times*, M1 kw, K1.

Rep inc row every 8 rows 11 (12, 12, 12) times. Rep final inc for Small on row 101 of main patt. Inc st will initially be a knit st in next patt row 1 rep. Inc in this patt can be a little confusing; to clarify and maintain `correct number of sts work as follows:

Row 13 (13, 17, 17): K2, work * to * of row 9 (9, 13, 13), K2.

Row 17 (17, 21, 21): K1, M1 kw, K1, work * to * of row 9 (9, 13, 13), K1, M1 kw, K1—48 (52, 54, 58) sts.

Row 21 (21, 25, 25): K3, work * to * of row 9 (9, 13, 13), K3.

Row 25 (25, 29, 29): K1, M1 kw, K2, work * to * of row 9 (9, 13, 13), K2, M1 kw, K1.

Row 29 (29, 33, 33): K1 (1, 2, 4), *K2tog 2 times, (K1, YO) 5 (6, 6, 6) times, K2tog 6 times, (K1, YO) 6 times, K2tog 6 times, (K1, YO) 5 (6, 6, 6) times, K2tog 2 times*, K1 (1, 2, 4)—50 (54, 56, 60) sts.

Row 33 (33, 37, 37): K1, M1 kw, K0 (0, 1, 3), work * to * of row 29 (29, 33, 33), K0 (0, 1, 3), M1 kw, K1.

Row 37 (37, 41, 41): K2 (2, 3, 5), work * to * of row 29 (29, 33, 33), K2 (2, 3, 5).

Row 41 (41, 45, 45): K1, M1 kw, K1 (1, 2, 4), work * to * of row 29 (29, 33, 33), K1 (1, 2, 4), M1 kw, K1—54 (58, 60, 64) sts.

Row 45 (45, 49, 49): K3 (3, 4, 6), work * to * of row 29 (29, 33, 33), K3 (3, 4, 6).

Row 49 (49, 53, 53): K1, M1 kw, K2 (2, 3, 5), work * to * of row 29 (29, 33, 33), K2 (2, 3, 5), M1 kw, K1.

Row 53 (53, 57, 57): K1 (3, 4, 6), *K2tog 3 times, (K1, YO) 6 times, K2tog 6 times, (K1, YO) 6 times, K2tog 3 times*, K1 (3, 4, 6).

Row 57 (57, 61, 61): K1, M1 kw, K0 (2, 3, 5), work * to * of row 53 (53, 57, 57), K0 (2, 3, 5), M1 kw, K1—58 (62, 64, 68) sts.

Row 61 (61, 65, 65): K2 (4, 5, 7), work * to * of row 53 (53, 57, 57), K2 (4, 5, 7).

Row 65 (65, 69, 69): K1, M1 kw, K1 (3, 4, 6), work * to * of row 53 (53, 57, 57), K1 (3, 4, 6), M1 kw, K1.

Row 69 (69, 73, 73): K3 (5, 6, 8), work * to * of row 53 (53, 57, 57), K3 (5, 6, 8)—60 (64, 66, 70) sts.

Row 73 (73, 77, 77): K1, M1 kw, K2 (4, 5, 7), work * to * of row 53 (53, 57, 57), K2 (4, 5, 7), M1 kw, K1.

Row 77 (77, 81, 81): K4 (6, 7, 9), work * to * of row 53 (53, 57, 57), K4 (6, 7, 9).

Row 81 (81, 85, 85): K1, M1 kw, K3 (5, 6, 8), work * to * of row 53 (53, 57, 57), K3 (5, 6, 8), M1 kw, K1.

Row 85 (85, 89, 89): K5 (7, 8, 10), work * to * of row 53 (53, 57, 57), K5 (7, 8, 10)—64 (68, 70, 74) sts.

Row 89 (89, 93, 93): K1, M1 kw, K4 (6, 7, 9), work * to * of row 53 (53, 57, 57), K4 (6, 7, 9), M1 kw, K1.

Row 93 (93, 97, 97): K6 (8, 9, 11), work * to * of row 53 (53, 57, 57), K6 (8, 9, 11).

Row 97 (97, 101, 101): K1, M1 kw, K5 (7, 8, 10), work * to * of row 53 (53, 57, 57), K5 (7, 8, 10), M1 kw, K1.

Row 101 (101, 105, 105): Work each size as follows:

    Small: K1, M1 kw, K6, work * to * of row 53, K6, M1 kw, K1.

    Medium: K9, work * to * of row 53, K9.

    Large: K10, work * to * of row 57, K10.

    Extra large: K12, work * to * of row 57, K12.

Row 105 (105, 109, 109): Work each size as follows:

    Small: K8, work as established, K8—70 sts.

    Medium: K1, M1 kw, K8, work * to * of row 53, K8, M1 kw, K1—74 sts.

    Large: K1, M1 kw, K9, work * to * of row 57, K9, M1 kw, K1—76 sts.

    Extra large: K1, M1 kw, K11, work * to * of row 57, K11, M1 kw, K1—80 sts.

Shape cap: When sleeve measures 13¾ (14¼,

14¾, 15¼)" and you have worked 108 (112, 116, 120) rows, BO 5 sts at beg of next 2 rows. Dec 1 st, then BO 2 sts at beg of next 2 rows—54 (58, 60, 64) sts. Then dec 1 st each edge EOR 16 times as follows:

Row 113 (117, 121, 125): K1 (3, 4, 6), K2tog 3 times, (K1, YO) 5 times, K2tog 6 times, (K1, YO) 6 times, K2tog 6 times, (K1, YO) 5 times, K2tog 3 times, K1 (3, 4, 6).

Row 115 (119, 123, 127) and all rem patt row 3 dec rows through row 143: K1, SSK, knit to last 3 sts, K2tog, K1—50 (54, 56, 60) sts on row 115 (119, 123, 127).

Row 117 (121, 125, 129): K2 (2, 3, 5), K2tog 2 times, (K1, YO) 4 (5, 5, 5) times, K2tog 6 times, (K1, YO) 6 times, K2tog 6 times, (K1, YO) 4 (5, 5, 5) times, K2tog 2 times, K2 (2, 3, 5).

Row 121 (125, 129, 133): K1 (2, 1, 3), K2tog 1 (2, 2, 2) times, (K1, YO) 4 (4, 5, 5) times, K2tog 6 times, (K1, YO) 6 times, K2tog 6 times, (K1, YO) 4 (4, 5, 5) times, K2tog 1 (2, 2, 2) times, K1 (2, 1, 3)—44 (48, 50, 54) sts.

Row 125 (129, 133, 137): K1 (1, 2, 4), K2tog, (K1, YO) 3 (4, 4, 4) times, K2tog 6 times, (K1, YO) 6 times, K2tog 6 times, (K1, YO) 3 (4, 4, 4) times. K2tog, K1 (1, 2, 4).

Row 129 (133, 137, 141): K2 (2, 3, 3), (K1, YO) 2 (3, 3, 4) times, K2tog 6 times, (K1, YO) 6 times, K2tog 6 times, (K1, YO) 2 (3, 3, 4) times, K2 (2, 3, 3)—36 (40, 42, 46) sts.

Row 133 (137, 141, 145): K2 (2, 3, 3), K2tog, (K1, YO) 1 (2, 2, 3) times, K2tog 5 times, (K1, YO) 6 times, K2tog 5 times, (K1, YO) 1 (2, 2, 3) times, K2tog, K2 (2, 3, 3)—32 (36, 38, 42) sts.

Row 137 (141, 145, 149): K3 (3, 4, 4), (K1,

YO) 0 (1, 1, 2) times, K2tog 5 times, (K1, YO) 6 times, K2tog 5 times, (K1, YO) 0 (1, 1, 2) times, K3 (3, 4, 4)—28 (32, 34, 38) sts.

Row 141 (145, 149, 153): K2 (2, 3, 3), (K1, YO) 0 (1, 1, 2) times, K2tog 4 times, (K1, YO) 6 times, K2tog 4 times, (K1, YO) 0 (1, 1, 2) times, K2 (2, 3, 3)—24 (28, 30, 34) sts.

Row 143 (for Small only): Work as row 115. (This is the last time you will work this dec on patt row 3.)

Rows 144–146 (for Small only): Dec 1 st at beg of rows 144 and 145 (knit all sts row 145). BO pw rem 20 sts.

For Medium, Large, and Extra Large, cont as established.

Row (149, 153, 157): K3 (4, 4), (K1, YO) 0 (0, 1) time, K2tog 3 times, (K1, YO) 6 times, K2tog 3 times, (K1, YO) 0 (0, 1) time, K3 (4, 4)—24 (26, 30) sts.

Rows 150–152 (for Medium only): Work as for Small, rows 144–146. BO pw rem 22 sts.

For Large and Extra Large, cont as established.

Row (157, 161): K3 (5), K2tog 3 times, (K1, YO) 6 times, K2tog 3 times, K3 (5)—24 (28) sts.

Rows 158–160 (for Large only): Work as for Small, rows 144–146. BO pw rem 22 sts.

Row 165 (for Extra Large only): K1, K2tog, K2, K2tog 3 times, (K1, YO) 6 times, K2tog 3 times, K2, K2tog, K1—26 sts.

Rows 166–168: Work as for size Small, rows 144–146. BO pw rem 24 sts.

Cardigan Finishing

- Block to measurements.
- Sew shoulder seams using invisible horizontal seaming (page 19).
- Sew side and underarm seams using combination of invisible vertical on St st (page 20) and invisible vertical on reverse St st seaming (page 20).
- **Neckband:** With smaller 40" needles, PU 6 sts per inch up first front edge, transfer back neck sts from holder, and PU sts down second front edge. Knit 3 rows and BO kw on next row.

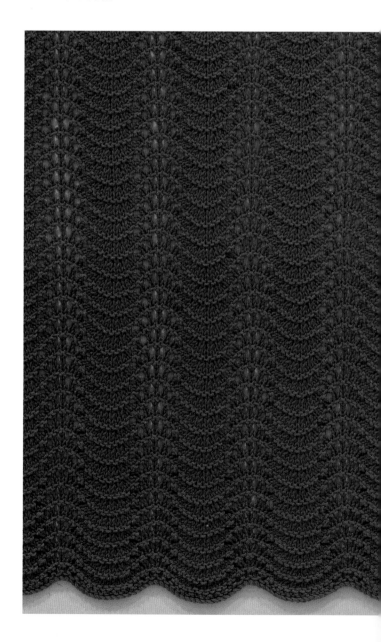

Shell Front

- With larger needles, cable CO 110 (116, 122, 128) sts. Knit 2 rows. Work 14 rows of ripple st patt as for cardigan back.
- **Next row:** Knit and dec 17 sts by working K2tog evenly spaced across row—93 (99, 105, 111) sts. Cont in St st until work measures 12 (12½, 13, 13½)" from beg.
- Shape armholes: BO 4 (4, 5, 5) sts at beg of next 2 rows. Dec 1 st, then BO 1 (2, 2, 2) sts at beg of next 2 rows. Dec 1 st, then BO 0 (0, 0, 1) st at beg of next 2 rows—79 (83, 87, 91) sts.
- Shape V-neck: Work across 39 (41, 43, 45) sts, join second ball of yarn and BO center st, finish row. Working both sides at same time with 2 separate balls of yarn, work dec row as follows: On RS, knit to within 3 sts of left neck edge, K2tog, K1; then at right neck edge, K1, SSK, knit to end of row. Rep dec row every 4 rows a total of 13 times—26 (28, 30, 32) sts on each side.
- Shape shoulders: Cont with 2 separate balls of yarn, when armhole depth measures 6½ (7, 7½, 8)", at beg of each side edge, BO 8 (9, 9, 10) sts once. Dec 1 st, then BO 7 (8, 9, 10) sts once. Dec 1 st, then BO 9 (9, 10, 10) sts once.

Shell Back

Work as for front, omitting V-neck shaping. After shaping shoulders, place rem 27 sts at center back neck on holder.

Shell Finishing

- Block to measurements.
- Sew shoulder seams using invisible horizontal seaming (page 19).
- Sew side seams using invisible vertical on St st seaming (page 20).

◆ **Neck edging:** With smaller 20" needles, PU 6 sts per inch along one side of neck, transfer back neck sts from holder, and PU sts down other neck edge. Knit 2 rows, and BO kw on next row. Sew overlap at center of V-neck in place.

◆ **Arm edging:** With smaller circular 20" needles, PU 6 sts per inch around armhole. Join and knit 2 rows, and BO kw on next row. Rep for second armhole edge.

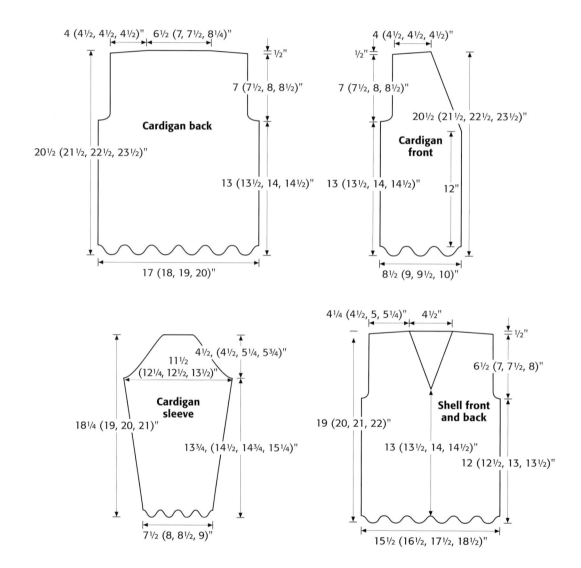

Feminine, fitted, and fun with a flair, the mock cable is simply a right twist, so no cable needle is required.

Since Flair Mock Cable Pullover is not blocked, the ribbing hugs the body. If you prefer a looser fit, you could block this sweater for more of a T-shirt feeling. After I wear this sweater, if I feel the ribbing has opened up more than I like it to, I simply lay it flat, spray it with a little warm water, scrunch it, and let it dry.

Skill Level:

◀▬■▭

Materials

- 9 (9, 10, 10) balls of Sesia Cable 2005 (100% mercerized cotton; 50 g; 147 yds), color 479 (1)
- Size 3 needles or size required to obtain gauge
- Size 3 circular needles (16")
- Size 2 circular needles (16")

Gauge

40½ sts and 36 rows = 4" in main patt st on size 3 needles unblocked, unstretched, and unpinned

Note: *Do not be misled by gauge or schematics. When you put the finished sweater on, the ribbing will open up and this sweater will mold to the shape of your body.*

Size: Petite (Small, Medium, Large)

Finished Measurements
Unblocked Bust: 22½ (24, 28, 31)"
Will Stretch to Bust: 31 (33, 35, 37)"
Length: 19½ (20½, 21½, 22½)"

Pattern Stitch

Right Twist (RT)

K2tog leaving sts on left needle, insert right needle between 2 sts just knit tog, and knit through front of first st again, then sl both sts from needle tog.

Back

- With larger needles, cable CO 210 (228, 264, 291) sts, and work rows 1–9 to create flair edge.

  Row 1 (RS): K1, P4, *K2, P7, rep from * to last 7 sts, K2, P4, K1.

  Rows 2 and 4: K5, *P2, K7, rep from * to last 7 sts, P2, K5.

  Row 3: K1, P4, *RT, P7, rep from * to last 7 sts, RT, P4, K1.

  Row 5: K1, P2, P2tog tbl, *K2, P2tog, P3, P2tog tbl, rep from * to last 7 sts, K2, P2tog, P2, K1—164 (178, 206, 227) sts.

  Rows 6 and 8: K4, *P2, K5, rep from * to last 6 sts, P2, K4.

  Row 7: K1, P3, *RT, P5, rep from * to last 6 sts, RT, P3, K1.

  Row 9: K1, P1, P2tog tbl, *K2, P2tog, P1, P2tog tbl, rep from * to last 6 sts, K2, P2tog, P1, K1—118 (128, 148, 163) sts.

- **Beg main patt as follows:**
  Row 1 and 3 (WS): K3, *P2, K3, rep from *.
  Row 2: K1, P2, *RT, P3, rep from * to last 5 sts, RT, P2, K1.
  Row 4: K1, P2, *K2, P3, rep from * to last 5 sts, K2, P2, K1.
  Cont until work measures 12½ (13, 13½, 14)" from beg.
- Shape armholes: BO 4 (4, 4, 5) sts at beg of next 2 rows. Dec 1 st, then BO 2 (2, 2, 3) sts at beg of next 2 rows—104 (114, 134, 145) sts. Cont in patt until work measures 18½ (19, 19½, 20)" from beg.
- Shape neck and shoulders: Work in patt across 31 (34, 39, 42) sts, attach 2nd ball of yarn, BO 42 (46, 56, 61) center sts, finish row. Work both sides at same time with 2 separate balls of yarn, at each neck edge on EOR, dec 1 st, then BO 1 st once. Dec 1 st on next 3 rows—26 (29, 34, 37) sts each shoulder. AT SAME TIME when armhole measures 6½ (7, 7½, 8)", at each shoulder edge, BO 8 (9, 10, 11) sts on EOR once. Dec 1 st, then BO 8 (9, 11, 12) sts on EOR twice.

Front

Work as for back except beg neck shaping when work measures 18 (18½, 19, 19½)".

Sleeves

- With larger needles, cable CO 93 (102, 120, 129) sts and work rows 1–9 to create flair edge as for back—53 (58, 68, 73) sts. Work 1" in main patt as for back. Cont in main patt, inc on RS rows by using M1 pw after first selvage st and before last st every 6 rows a total of 16 (17, 14, 14) times, then every 4 rows 0 (0, 6, 7) times—85 (92, 108, 115) sts.
- Cont in patt until work measures 12½ (13, 13½, 14)".

- **Shape cap:** BO 4 (4, 5, 5) sts at beg of next 2 rows. Dec 1 st, then BO 2 (2, 2, 3) sts at beg of next 2 rows. Dec 1 st each edge on next 1 (1, 2, 2) row(s). Dec 1 st each edge EOR 10 (11, 10, 11) times. Dec 1 st each edge on next 9 (11, 13, 15) rows. Dec 1 st, then BO 1 (1, 1, 1) st at beg of next 2 rows. Dec 1 st, then BO 2 (1, 2, 2) sts at beg of next 2 rows. Dec 1 st, then BO 2 (2, 4, 3) sts at beg of next 2 rows. BO rem 15 (18, 22, 23) sts in patt.

Finishing

- Do not block since work needs to retain its elasticity and resilience.
- Sew shoulder seams matching patt sts using invisible horizontal seaming (page 19).
- Set in sleeves using invisible vertical to horizontal seaming (page 19).
- Sew side and underarm seams using invisible vertical on reverse St st seaming (page 20).
- **Neck edging:** With RS of garment facing you, and smaller circular needles, PU 7 sts per inch around neck edge. With larger circular needles, purl 2 rnds, and BO pw on next rnd.

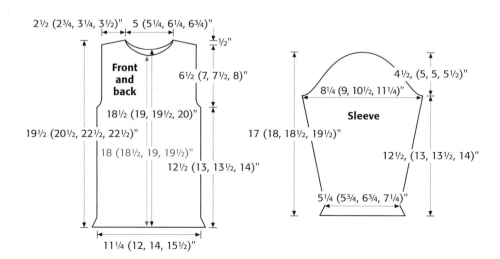

Front and back: 2½ (2¾, 3¼, 3½)" 5 (5¼, 6¼, 6¾)" ½" 6½ (7, 7½, 8)" 18½ (19, 19½, 20)" 19½ (20½, 22½, 22½)" 18 (18½, 19, 19½)" 12½ (13, 13½, 14)" 11¼ (12, 14, 15½)"

Sleeve: 4½, (5, 5, 5½)" 8¼ (9, 10½, 11¼)" 17 (18, 18½, 19½)" 12½, (13, 13½, 14)" 5¼ (5¾, 6¾, 7¼)"

Cabled Hearts V-Neck Pullover

"Close to the heart" describes the easy and clever way the V neckline nestles into the Cabled Heart pattern in this design. The sweater is rich in texture in a sculptural way, with strong diagonal lines as well as vertical lines in the main patterns that are sure to engage the eye. The ribbing is a unique cable application. The sleeves are bracelet length.

Skill Level:

Materials

- 8 (8, 9, 9) skeins of Tahki Cotton Classic (100% mercerized cotton; 50 g; 108 yds), color 3802
- Size 6 needles or size required to obtain gauge
- Size 4 needles
- Cable needle

Gauge

25 sts and 28 rows = 4" in main patt sts on size 6 needles when blocked

Pattern Stitches

Cabled Heart

Multiple of 37 sts; number of sts will vary in some rows.

T9FP (Twist 9 Front Purl) = sl 4 sts to cn and hold at front of work, K4, P1, K4 from cn.

Size: Small (Medium, Large, Extra Large)

Finished Measurements
Bust: 36½ (38½, 40½, 42½)"
Length: 21¼ (21¾, 22¼, 22¼)"

C4B (Cable 4 Back) = sl 2 sts to cn and hold at back of work, K2, K2 from cn.

C4F (Cable 4 Front) = sl 2 sts to cn and hold at front of work, K2, K2 from cn.

C12XR (Cable 12X Right) = sl 8 sts to cn and hold at back of work, K4, sl 4 sts from cn back to left needle and knit these 4 sts, K4 from cn.

C12XL (Cable 12X Left) = sl 8 sts to cn and hold at front of work, K4, sl 4 sts from cn back to left needle and knit these 4 sts, K4 sts from cn.

Row 1 (RS): *P2, K4*, rep from * to * twice, P1, **K4, P2**, rep from ** to ** twice.

Row 2: *K2, P4*, rep from * to * twice, K1, **P4, K2**, rep from ** to ** twice.

Row 3: P2, K4, P2, C4F, P2, K4, P1, K4, P2, C4B, P2, K4, P2.

Row 4: Rep row 2.

Rows 5 and 6: Rep rows 1 and 2.

Row 7: P2, K4, P2, C4F, P2, T9FP, P2, C4B, P2, K4, P2.

Row 8: Rep row 2.

Row 9: P2, M1 pw, *K4, P2*, rep from * to * once, K4, M1 pw, P1, M1 pw, **K4, P2**, rep from ** to ** once, K4, M1 pw, P2—41 sts.

Row 10: K3, *P4, K2*, rep from * to * once, P4, K3, **P4, K2**, rep from ** to ** once, P4, K3.

Row 11: P3, M1 pw, K4, P2tog, C4F, P2tog, K4, M1 pw, P3, M1 pw, K4, P2tog, C4B, P2tog, K4, M1 pw, P3.

Row 12: K4, *P4, K1*, rep from * to * once, P4, K5, **P4, K1**, rep from ** to ** once, P4, K4.

Row 13: P4, M1 pw, K3, sl 1, K1, psso, K4, K2tog, K3, M1 pw, P5, M1 pw, K3, sl 1, K1, psso, K4, K2tog, K3, M1 pw, P4.

Row 14: K5, P12, K7, P12, K5.

Row 15: P5, M1 pw, K4, C4F, K4, M1 pw, P7, M1 pw, K4, C4B, K4, M1 pw, P5—45 sts.

Row 16: K6, P12, K9, P12, K6.

Row 17: P6, C12XR, P9, C12XL, P6.

Row 18: Rep row 16.

Row 19: P4, P2tog, K4, C4F, K4, P2tog, P5, P2tog, K4, C4B, K4, P2tog, P4—41 sts.

Row 20: Rep row 14.

Row 21: P3, P2tog, *K4, M1 pw*, rep from * to * once, K4, P2tog, P3, P2tog, **K4, M1 pw**, rep from ** to ** once, K4, P2tog, P3.

Row 22: Rep row 12.

Row 23: P2, P2tog, K4, M1 pw, P1, C4F, P1, M1 pw, K4, P2tog, P1, P2tog, K4, M1 pw, P1, C4B, P1, M1 pw, K4, P2tog, P2.

Row 24: Rep row 10.

Row 25: P1, P2tog, *K4, P2*, rep from * to * once, K4, P3tog, **K4, P2**, rep from ** to ** once, K4, P2tog, P1—37 sts.

Row 26: Rep row 2.

Row 27: Rep row 7.

Row 28: Rep row 2.

Rep these 28 rows for patt.

Diamond with Cable Pattern

Multiple of 16 sts

T4R (Twist 4 Right) = sl 1 st to cn and hold at back of work, K3, P1 from cn.

T4L (Twist 4 Left) = sl 3 sts to cn and hold at front of work, P1, K3 from cn.

C6B (Cable 6 Back) = sl 3 sts to cn and hold at back of work, K3, K3 from cn.

C6F (Cable 6 Front) = sl 3 sts to cn and hold at front of work, K3, K3 from cn.

Row 1 (RS): P5, K6, P5.

Row 2: K5, P6, K5.

Row 3: P5, C6B, P5. Note that this row will be C6B on right side of work and C6F on left side of back, front, and sleeve.

Row 4: Rep row 2.

Row 5: P4, T4R, T4L, P4.

Row 6: K4, P3, K2, P3, K4.

Row 7: P3, T4R, P2, T4L, P3.

Row 8: K3, P3, K4, P3, K3.

Row 9: P2, T4R, P4, T4L, P2.

Row 10: K2, P3, K6, P3, K2.

Row 11: P1, T4R, P6, T4L, P1.

Row 12: K1, P3, K8, P3, K1.

Row 13: T4R, P8, T4L.

Row 14: P3, K10, P3.

Row 15: T4L, P8, T4R.

Row 16: Rep row 12.

Row 17: P1, T4L, P6, T4R, P1.

Row 18: Rep row 10.

Row 19: P2, T4L, P4, T4R, P2.

Row 20: Rep row 8.

Row 21: P3, T4L, P2, T4R, P3.

Row 22: Rep row 6.

Row 23: P4, T4L, T4R, P4.

Rows 24–26: Rep rows 2–4.

Rows 27 and 28: Rep rows 1 and 2.

Rep these 28 rows for patt.

Eccentric Cable

Multiple of 8 sts.

C8B (Cable 8 Back) = sl 4 sts to cn and hold at back of work, K4, K4 from cn.

C8F (Cable 8 Front) = sl 4 sts to cn and hold at front of work, K4, K4 from cn.

Row 1 (RS): K8.

Row 2: P8.

Row 3: C8B. Note that this row will be C8B on right-hand side of work and C8F on left-hand side of back, front, and sleeve.

Row 4: Rep row 2.

Rows 5–12: Rep rows 1 and 2 twice, then rep rows 1–4 once.

Rows 13–28: Rep rows 1 and 2 another 8 times.

Rep these 28 rows for patt.

Back

- With smaller needles, cable CO 110 (116, 122, 128) sts and work bottom ribbing as follows:

  Row 1 (RS): *P2, K4, rep from * to last 2 sts, P2.

  Row 2: *K2, P4, rep from * to last 2 sts, K2.

  Row 3: *P2, C4F, rep from * to last 2 sts, P2.

Row 4: Rep row 2.

Rows 5–10: Rep rows 1 and 2.

Row 11: Rep row 3.

Next row (WS): Purl all sts and inc 5 sts evenly spaced across row by using M1 pw—115 (121, 127, 133) sts.

- Change to larger needles. Establish main patts as follows:

  Row 1 (RS): K1, P2 (5, 8, 9), work 8 sts in eccentric cable (row 1), P2 (2, 2, 3), work 16 sts in diamond with cable patt (row 1), P2 (2, 2, 3), work 8 sts in eccentric cable, work 37 sts in cabled heart patt (row 1), work 8 sts in eccentric cable, P2 (2, 2, 3), work 16 sts in diamond with cable patt, P2 (2, 2, 3), work 8 sts in eccentric cable, P2 (5, 8, 9), K1.

Work even in established patts for a total of 89 rows in main patts and work measures approx 13¾" from beg (includes 12 rows of bottom ribbing)—101 total rows.

- Shape armholes: BO 3 (3, 4, 4) sts at beg of next 2 rows. Dec 1 st, then BO 1 (1, 2, 2) sts at beg of next 2 rows—105 (111, 113, 119) sts. Work even to armhole depth of 6½ (7, 7½, 7½)". Note that after armhole shaping, for Small only, the 8-st eccentric cable at beg and end of row will become a 5-st eccentric cable preceded and followed by selvage st of K1. For 5-st eccentric cable, C5B = sl 3 sts to cn and hold at back of work, K2, K3 from cn; C5F = sl 2 sts to cn and hold at front of work, K3, K2 from cn.

- Shape shoulders: BO 9 (10, 10, 11) sts at beg of next 2 rows. Dec 1 st, then BO 9 (9, 10, 11) sts at beg of next 2 rows. Dec 1 st, then BO 9 (11, 11, 12) sts at beg of next 2 rows. BO rem 47 neck sts and incorporate K2tog 10 times evenly across this row to keep back neck edge close to neck.

Front

♦ Work as for back with exception of neck shaping, which will beg on row 93 of main patt sts. Note that row 93 = row 9 of cabled heart patt, and that both sides of neck are worked at same time with 2 separate balls of yarn.

Row 93: Dec 1 center st working K2tog and do not M1 pw on either side of center st; attach 2nd ball of yarn and work to end of row—19 sts on each side in cabled heart patt.

Note: The 4 sts on either side of neck edge will be K4 on all RS rows and P4 on all WS rows for rest of front. The following rows address neck shaping within cabled heart patt. Work diamond cable and eccentric cable patts as established on either side of cabled heart patt.

Row 95: Omit center M1 pw, P3, M1 pw.

Row 97: Omit center M1 pw, P5, M1 pw.

Row 99: Omit center M1 pw, P7, M1 pw.

Row 101: On C12XR and C12XL, dec 2 sts at each neck edge (inside of K4) working K2tog twice.

Row 103: P4, P2tog, K2, C4F (sl 2 sts to cn and hold in front, K2tog twice, K2 from cn), K2, neck opening, K2, C4B (sl 4 sts to cn and hold in back K2, then from cn K2tog twice), K2, P2tog, P4.

Row 105: (Left side front) P3, P2tog, K5, K2tog, K1, neck opening, (right side front) K1, K2tog, K5, P2tog, P3.

Row 107: P2, P2tog, K4, K2tog, K1, neck opening, K1, K2tog, K4, P2tog, P2.

Row 109: P1, P2tog, K3, K2tog, K1, neck opening, K1, K2tog, K3, P2tog, P1.

Row 111: P2, K2, K2tog, K1, neck opening, K1, K2tog, K2, P2.

Row 113: After 16 sts in diamond with cable patt, P2, K6, K2tog, P2, K4, neck opening, K4, P2, K2tog, K6, P2, cont in diamond and cable patt.

Row 115: After 16 sts in diamond with cable patt, P2, C7B (sl 4 sts to cn and hold in back, K3, K4 from cn), P2, K4, neck opening, K4, P2, C7F (sl 3 sts to cn and hold in front, K4, K3 from cn), P2, cont in diamond with cable patt.

Row 117: After 16 sts in diamond with cable patt, P2, K5, K2tog, P2, K4, neck opening, K4, P2, K2tog, K5, P2, cont in diamond with cable patt.

Row 119: Work even without decs.

Row 121: After 16 sts in diamond with cable patt, P2, K4, K2tog, P2, K4, neck opening, K4, P2, K2tog, K4, P2, cont in diamond with cable patt.

Row 123: Work even without decs. Note that C7B and C7F from row 115 will become C5B and C5F. C5B = sl 3 sts to cn and hold in back, K2, K3 from cn. C5F = sl 2 sts to cn and hold in front, K3, K2 from cn.

Row 125: After 16 sts in diamond with cable patt, P2, K3, K2tog, P2, K4, neck opening, K4, P2, K2tog, K3, P2, cont in diamond with cable patt.

Row 127: Work even without decs.

Row 129: After 16 sts in diamond with cable patt, P2, K2, K2tog, P2, K4, neck opening, K4, P2, K2tog, K2, P2, cont in diamond with cable patt.

+ Work even until armhole depth is same as for back. Work shoulder shaping as for back. Keep rem K4, P2 at neck edges on needles and knit for approx 3½" to meet at center of back of neck. BO rem 6 sts.

Sleeves

+ With smaller needles, cable CO 50 (50, 56, 56) sts and work bottom ribbing rows 1–11, as for back.
  Row 12: Purl all sts, inc 3 sts evenly spaced across this row using M1 pw—53 (53, 59, 59) sts.
+ Change to larger needles and work main patt as follows:
  Row 1 (RS): P0 (0, 3, 3), 8 sts in eccentric cable, 37 sts in cabled heart patt, 8 sts in eccentric cable, P0 (0, 3, 3).
+ **Shape sleeve:** Beg with row 5, inc 1 st each edge working M1 pw or M1 kw as appropriate to patt after first selvage st and before last selvage st every 4 rows a total of 20 times. AT SAME TIME when you have worked incs to 71 sts, beg to introduce diamond with cable patt at edge (for sizes Small

and Medium, work row 37 of main patt as K1, M1 pw, K3, P4, cont to last 8 sts, end P4, K3, M1 pw, K1; for sizes Medium and Large, work row 25 of main patt as K1, M1 kw, K3, P3, cont to last 7 sts, end P3, K3, M1 pw, K1). Cont to work inc in patt as it becomes appropriate—93 (93, 99, 99) sts.

+ **Shape cap:** When work measures 13¾" from beg, approx row 89 of main patt, BO 3 (3, 4, 4) sts at beg of next 2 rows. Dec 1 st, then BO 1 (1, 2, 2) sts at beg of next 2 rows. Dec 1 st each edge EOR next 0 (0, 4, 4) times. Dec 1 st each edge on each row next 24 (24, 20, 20) rows. Dec 1 st, then BO 1 st at beg of next 4 rows. BO rem 27 (27, 29, 29) sts.

Finishing

+ Meticulously block to measurements.
+ Sew shoulder seams, matching patt sts using invisible horizontal seaming (page 19).
+ Sew center back of neck seam on neck edging using invisible horizontal seaming (page 19).
+ Sew neck edging in place to back of neck using whipstitch.
+ Set in sleeves using invisible vertical to horizontal seaming (page 19).
+ Sew side and underarm seams using invisible vertical on reverse St st seaming (page 19).

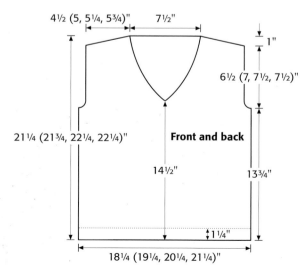

4½ (5, 5¼, 5¾)"   7½"

1"

6½ (7, 7½, 7½)"

21¼ (21¾, 22¼, 22¼)"   **Front and back**

14½"

13¾"

1¼"

18¼ (19¼, 20¼, 21¼)"

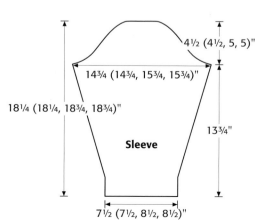

4½ (4½, 5, 5)"

14¾ (14¾, 15¾, 15¾)"

18¼ (18¼, 18¾, 18¾)"

13¾"

Sleeve

7½ (7½, 8½, 8½)"

Classic Cable and Corded Rib Turtleneck

Size: Small (Medium, Large,
Extra Large)

Finished Measurements
Bust: 35 (37, 39, 41)"
Length: 21½ (22½, 23½, 24½)"

Classic, timeless style—brought up to date

with fold-back cuffs and a bright color—

makes this a sweater to wear and enjoy

for many years. Charming braids and

cord-like cables are both intricate and simple

with slightly understated and delicate tones.

Skill Level:

■■■◻

Materials

+ 9 (10, 10, 11) skeins of Jaeger Matchmaker
  Merino 4 ply (100% wool; 50 g; 200 yds),
  color 712
+ Size 3 needles or size required to obtain
  gauge
+ Size 2 circular needles (16")
+ Size 2 straight needles

Gauge

32 sts and 36 rows = 4" in main patt sts on size
3 needles when blocked

Main Pattern Stitches

Corded Rib

Multiple of 2 sts
Row 1 (RS): Sl 1 pw, K1, YO, psso the K1 and YO.
Row 2: P2.
Rep these 2 rows for patt.

Alternating Cable

Multiple of 6 sts
C4B (Cable 4 Back) = sl 2 sts to cn and hold at
    back of work, K2, K2 from cn.
C4F (Cable 4 Front) = sl 2 sts to cn and hold at
    front of work, K2, K2 from cn.

Row 1 (RS): C4B, K2.
Rows 2 and 4: P6.
Row 3: K2, C4F.
Rep these 4 rows for patt.

Multiple of 9 sts
C6B (Cable 6 Back)= sl 3 sts to cn and hold at
    back of work, K3, K3 from cn.
C6F (Cable 6 Front) = sl 3 sts to cn and hold at
    front of work, K3, K3 from cn.

Row 1 (RS): C6B, K3.
Rows 2 and 4: P9.
Row 3: C6F, K3.
Rep these 4 rows for patt.

72 Classic Cable and Corded Rib Turtleneck

Back

- With smaller needles, cable CO 142 (150, 158, 166) sts, and work bottom ribbing as follows:

  Row 1 (RS): K1, *P2, sl 1 pw, K1, YO, psso the K1 and YO, rep from * to last st, K1.

  Row 2: K1, *P2, K2, rep from * to last st, K1.

  Rep rows 1 and 2 for a total of 18 rows; approx 2".

- Change to larger needles and establish main patts as follows:

  Row 1 (RS): K2, (P2, 2 sts in corded rib) 1 (2, 3, 4) times, K3, (2 sts in corded rib, P2) twice, K6, (P2, 2 sts in corded rib) twice, K3, (2 sts in corded rib, P2) twice, K6, (P2, 2 sts in corded rib) twice, K3, (2 sts in corded rib, P2) twice, K4, M1 kw, K4, (P2, 2 sts in corded rib) twice, K3, (2 sts in corded rib, P2) twice, K6, (P2, 2 sts in corded rib) twice, K3, (2 sts in corded rib, P2) twice, K6, (P2, 2 sts in corded rib) twice, K3, (2 sts in corded rib, P2) 1 (2, 3, 4) times, K2—143 (151, 159, 167) sts.

  Rows 2, 4, and 6: Knit all knit sts and purl all purl sts.

  Row 3: Rep row 1 working row 1 of alternating cable for all K6 and K9.

  Row 5: Rep row 1 working row 3 of alternating cable for all K6 and K9.

  Rep rows 3–6 until work measures 14 (14½, 15, 15½)" from beg.

- **Shape armholes:** BO 5 (5, 5, 6) sts at beg of next 2 rows. Dec 1 st, then BO 2 (2, 2, 3) sts at beg of next 2 rows—127 (135, 143, 147) sts rem. Work even until back measures 20½ (21½ 22½, 23½)" from beg, end with completed WS row.

- **Shape shoulders and neck:** BO 8 (9, 9, 10) sts at beg of next row, work in patt across 43 (46, 49, 50) sts, attach second ball of yarn and BO center 25 (25, 27, 27) sts for neck, finish row. Work both sides at same time. With 1 ball of yarn, BO 8 (9, 9, 10) sts at shoulder edge, and with other ball of yarn dec 1 st, then BO 6 (6, 7, 7) sts at beg of neck edge of same row. Cont in this manner with 2 balls of yarn, on next row, dec 1 st, then BO 8 (9, 9, 10) sts at shoulder edge, and dec 1 st, then BO 6 (6, 7, 7) sts at beg of neck edge. On next row dec 1 st, then BO 8 (9, 9, 10) sts at shoulder edge, and dec 1 st, then BO 4 sts at beg of neck edge. On next row dec 1 st, then BO 8 (9, 10, 10) sts at shoulder edge, and dec 1 st, then BO 4 sts at beg of neck edge. On next row, dec 1 st, then BO 8 (9, 10, 10) sts at shoulder edge, and dec 1 st, then BO 2 sts at beg of neck edge. On next row, dec 1 st, then BO 9 (10, 11, 11) sts at shoulder edge, and dec 1 st, then BO 2 sts at beg of neck edge. On next row, dec 1 st, then BO 9 (10, 11, 11) sts at shoulder edge.

Front

+ Work as for back, cont past armhole shaping until front measures 19¼ (20¼, 21¼, 22¼)" from beg, end with completed WS row.
+ **Shape neck:** Work in patt across 51 (55, 58, 60) sts, attach 2nd ball of yarn and BO center 25 (25, 27, 27) sts, finish rows. Work both sides at same time with 2 separate balls of yarn, at beg of each neck edge on EOR, dec 1 st, then BO 6 sts once. Dec 1 st, then BO 3 (3, 4, 4) sts once. Dec 1 st, then BO 1 st once. Dec 1 st twice. On last row of neck shaping beg shoulder shaping as for back.

Sleeves

+ With smaller needles, cable CO 68 (70, 72, 74) sts and work ribbing as for back beg with WS row instead of RS to create fold back cuff. Work a total of 36 rows.
+ Change to larger needles and establish main patts as follows:

   Transition Row (WS): K1 (2, 3, 4), P2, K2, P6, K2, P2, K2, P7, K2, P2, K2, P4, M1 pw, P4, K2, P2, K2, P7, K2, P2, K2, P6, K2, P2, K1 (2, 3, 4)–69 (71, 73, 75) sts.

   Row 1: K1, P0 (1, 2, 3), 2 sts in corded rib, P2, K6, (P2, 2 sts in corded rib) twice, K3, (2 sts in corded rib, P2) twice, K9, (P2, 2 sts in corded rib) twice, K3, (2 sts in corded rib, P2) twice, K6, P2, 2 sts in corded rib, P0 (1, 2, 3), K1.

   Rows 2, 4, and 6: Knit all knit sts and purl all purl sts.

   Row 3: Rep row 2 working row 1 of alternating cable for all K6 and K9.

Row 5: Rep row 2 working row 3 of alternating cable for all K6 and K9. Note that row 6 will be first sleeve inc row. See sleeve shaping below.

Rep rows 3–6. Note that as incs allow, work sts in patt as for back.

◆ **Shape sleeve:** On row 6, inc 1 st each edge as follows: K1, M1, cont in patt to last st, M1, K1. Work incs at each edge every 6 rows 19 (22, 23, 24) times more, then every 8 rows 2 (0, 0, 0) times—113 (117, 121, 125) sts; 145 (149, 153, 157) rows in main patts.

◆ **Shape cap:** BO 5 (5, 5, 6) sts at beg of next 2 rows. Dec 1 st, then BO 2 (2, 2, 3) sts at beg of next 2 rows. Using K2tog tbl for first 2 sts and K2tog for last 2 sts, dec 1 st at each edge EOR 1 (3, 6, 11) times. Dec 1 st at each edge 31 (31, 29, 23) times. Dec 1 st, then BO 2 sts at beg of next 2 rows. Dec 1 st, then BO 3 (3, 3, 4) sts at beg of next 2 rows. BO rem 19 (19, 21, 21) sts.

Finishing

◆ Meticulously block to measurements.
◆ Sew shoulder seams using invisible horizontal seaming (page 19).
◆ Set in sleeves using invisible vertical to horizontal seaming (page 19).
◆ Sew side seams and underarm seams using invisible vertical on reverse St st seaming (page 20).
◆ **Collar:** With smaller circular needles, PU 132 (132, 140, 140) sts from right to left and start with WS row, because RS will be facing inward (like cuff) due to fold. Work in ribbing as for back for 60 rows (approx 6") and BO in patt.

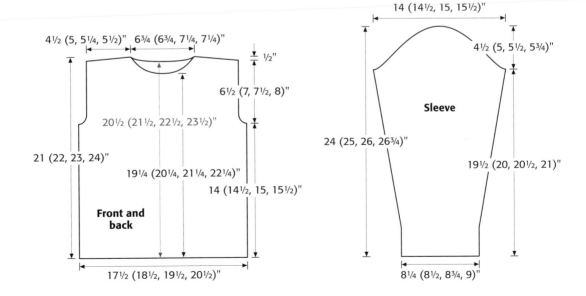

Front and back — 4½ (5, 5¼, 5½)"   6¾ (6¾, 7¼, 7¼)"   ½"   6½ (7, 7½, 8)"   20½ (21½, 22½, 23½)"   21 (22, 23, 24)"   19¼ (20¼, 21¼, 22¼)"   14 (14½, 15, 15½)"   17½ (18½, 19½, 20½)"

Sleeve — 14 (14½, 15, 15½)"   4½ (5, 5½, 5¾)"   24 (25, 26, 26¾)"   19½ (20, 20½, 21)"   8¼ (8½, 8¾, 9)"

Dollar Cable Cardigan

This very wearable, fitted cardigan in fingering-weight yarn may appear complex at first look, but there are only 2 rows of the 10-row dollar cable pattern that require the use of the cable needle. One of my favorite details is the collar with its vintage feel and comfort around the neck. It could just as easily be knit without the collar if you prefer and finished with the ribbing used on the front button-side edge.

Skill Level:

◀ ■ ■ ▢

Materials

+ 11 (12, 13, 14) balls of Sesia Cable 2005 (100% cotton; 50 g; 147 yds) color 972 **1**
+ Size 3 needles or size required to obtain gauge
+ Size 2 needles
+ Cable needle
+ 10 (11, 12, 12) buttons, approximately ½" diameter

Gauge

28 sts and 36 rows = 4" in main patt sts on size 3 needles when blocked

Size: Small (Medium, Large, Extra Large)

Finished Measurements
Bust: 36¼ (38, 41, 43½)"
Length: 21¾ (22¾, 23¾, 24¾)"

Main Pattern Stitches

Dollar Cable

Multiple of 12 sts

Row 1 (WS): K2, sl 1 wyif, P6, sl 1 wyif, K2.

Row 2: P2, sl next st to cn and hold in front, P3, K1 from cn; sl 3 sts to cn and hold in back, K1, P3 from cn; P2.

Row 3: K5, P2, K5.

Row 4: P2, sl next 3 sts to cn and hold in back, K1, K3 from cn; sl next st to cn and hold in front, K3, K1 from cn; P2.

Rows 5, 7, and 9: K2, P8, K2.

Rows 6, 8, and 10: P2, K8, P2.

Rep these 10 rows for patt.

Little Hourglass Rib

Multiple of 2 sts

Row 1 (WS): P2.

Row 2: K2tog tbl, knit same 2 sts tog again through front loops.

Row 3: P1, YO, P1.

Row 4: SSK, K1.

Rep these 4 rows for patt.

Cross-Stitch Rib

Multiple of 2 sts

Row 1 (WS): P2.

Row 2: Sk 1 st and knit into 2nd st, knit into skipped st, sl both sts from needle tog.

Rep these 2 rows for patt.

Back

- With smaller needles, cable CO 128 (138, 148, 158) sts and work bottom ribbing as follows:

Row 1 (WS): K3, *P2, K3, rep from *.

Row 2: K1 (selvage st), P2, *2 sts in cross-stitch rib, P3, 2 sts in little hourglass rib, P3, rep from * to last 5 sts, 2 sts in cross-stitch rib, P2, K1 (selvage st).

Rep rows 1 and 2 for a total of 18 rows.

- Change to larger needles. Establish main patts as follows:

Row 1 (WS): Work 18 (23, 28, 33) sts in established ribbing (you will be working a row 3 in little hourglass rib, which has YO and it will appear for that row that you have more sts than you need), 12 sts in dollar cable (row 1), 18 sts as established, 12 sts in dollar cable, 8 sts as established, 12 sts in dollar cable, 18 sts as established, 12 sts in dollar cable, work 18 (23, 28, 33) sts in established ribbing.

Cont in main patts as established in row 1 until 105 (110, 114, 119) rows have been worked: total 123 (128, 133, 138) rows including 18 rows of bottom ribbing. Work will measure approx 13¾ (14¼, 14¾, 15¼)".

- **Shape armholes:** Beg on main patts row 106 (111, 115, 120), BO 4 (5, 6, 7) sts at beg of next 2 rows. Dec 1 st, then BO 2 (3, 4, 5) sts at beg of next 2 rows—114 (120, 126, 132) sts. Work even through main patt row 175 (183, 192, 201) for armhole depth of 7½ (8, 8½, 9)".

- **Shape shoulders:** BO 10 (11, 12, 13) sts at beg of next 2 rows. Dec 1 st, then BO 10 (11, 11, 12) sts at beg of next 2 rows. Dec 1 st, then BO 11 (12, 12, 13) sts at beg of next 2 rows. BO rem 48 (48, 52, 52) sts.

Front

Directions are written for right side of front and must be reversed for left side.

- With smaller needles, cable CO 60 (65, 70, 75) sts and work bottom ribbing as follows:
  Row 1 (WS): K4, *P2, K3, rep from * to last st, K1.
  Row 2: K1 (selvage st), *P3, 2 sts in cross-stitch rib and cont to work ribbing as for back, alternating little hourglass and cross-stitch ribs between purl sts to last 6 sts, last 2 rib sts will be in cross-stitch rib for sizes Small and Large, and in little hourglass ribbing for sizes Medium and Extra Large, end all sizes with P3, K1 (selvage st).
  Cont bottom ribbing as established for a total of 18 rows.
- Change to larger needles. Establish main patts as follows:
  Row 1 (WS): K4, *P2, K3, rep from * 0 (1, 2, 3) times, 12 sts in dollar cable (row 1), 18 sts as established, 12 sts in dollar cable, K3, P2, K4.
  Cont in patt as established until same length as back to armhole.
- **Shape armholes:** Work armhole decs at side edge as for back—53 (56, 59, 62) sts. Cont in

patt as established until work measures 19½ (20½, 21½, 22½)" from beg, approx rows 158/159 for Small; rows 166/167 for Medium; rows 176/177 for Large; rows 184/185 for Extra Large. Row numbers are given as left front and WS/right front and RS.

- **Shape neck and shoulder:** At each neck edge, BO 4 (4, 6, 6) sts once. Dec 1 st, then BO 2 sts 3 times. Dec 1 st, then BO 1 st 3 times. Dec 1 st once. AT SAME TIME, shape shoulder at side edge as for back.

Sleeves

- With smaller needles, cable CO 58 (60, 62, 64) sts and work bottom ribbing as follows:
  Row 1 (WS): K3 (4, 5, 6) *P2, K3, rep from * to last 0 (1, 2, 3) sts, K0 (1, 2, 3).
  Row 2: K1 (selvage st), P2 (3, 4, 5), *2 sts in cross-stitch rib, P3, 2 sts in little hourglass rib, P3, rep from * to last 5 (6, 7, 8) sts, 2 sts in cross-stitch rib, P2 (3, 4, 5), K1 (selvage st).

Cont bottom ribbing as established for a total of 18 rows. On row 18 (RS), M1 pw after first st (selvage) and before last st (selvage)—60 (62, 64, 66) sts.

- **Shape sleeve:** Change to larger needles. Establish main patts as follows:

    Row 1 (WS): K4 (5, 6, 7), 2 sts in cross-stitch rib, K3, 12 sts in dollar cable, K3, 2 sts in cross-stitch rib, K3, 2 sts in little hourglass rib, K3, 2 sts in cross-stitch rib, K3, 12 sts in dollar cable, K3, 2 sts in cross-stitch rib, K4 (5, 6, 7). Cont in patt, beg on row 8 inc 1 st at each edge by using M1 pw after first selvage st and before last selvage st every 6 rows 20 (21, 21, 22) times—100 (104, 106, 110) sts.

- AT SAME TIME for all sizes, when there are 7 knit sts at beg and end of WS row, work these stitches as K2, P2, K3 at beg of row and as K3, P2, K2 at end of row to establish little hourglass rib from this point on for the P2 sts and so that incs are worked in patt. Second time that st incs allow, add cross-stitch rib at edge in same manner. Work even until sleeve measures 16½ (17, 17½, 18)" from beg, approx row 150 (154, 158, 162) from beg (including 18 rows of bottom ribbing).

- **Shape cap:** BO 4 (5, 6, 7) sts at beg of next 2 rows. Dec 1 st, then BO 2 (3, 4, 5) sts at beg of next 2 rows. Dec 1 st at beg of next 14 (24, 28, 34) rows. Work 0 (0, 3, 4) rows even. Dec 1 st at each edge on next 19 (13, 11, 8) rows. Dec 1 st, then BO 2 (2, 1, 1) sts at beg of next 2 rows. Dec 1 st, then BO 3 (3, 2, 1) sts at beg of next 2 rows. BO rem 20 (22, 24, 26) sts. Note that you should omit YO in row 3 of little hourglass rib if it occurs in last 2 rows of work.

Collar

Collar is worked in 2 sizes, Small/Medium (Large/Extra Large).

- With smaller needles, cable CO 20 sts. Purl selvage st on WS and knit selvage st on RS. Work ribbing as follows:

    Row 1 (WS): P1, (K3, P2) 3 times, K3, P1.

    Row 2 (RS): K1, P1, M1 pw, P2, 2 sts in cross-stitch rib, P3, 2 sts in little hourglass rib, P3, 2 sts in cross-stitch rib, P2, M1 pw, P1, K1.

Cont in ribbing working inc at each edge of each RS row between second and third st from edges and incorporating alternating rib patts as inc allows; except on row 6 where an inc must be worked between first and second st to incorporate rib patt. Remember the YO in row 7 in little hourglass rib.

Rep rows 1 and 2 for a total of 18 (20) rows—38 (40) sts.

◆ Change to larger needles. Establish main patts as follows:

Row 1 (WS): P1 (2), M1 kw, sl 1 wyif, P6, sl 1 wyif, K4, P2, K3, P1, YO, P1, K3, P2, K4, sl 1 wyif, P6, sl 1 wyif, M1 kw, P1 (2)—40 (42) sts.

Row 2: K1 (2), P1f&b, sl next st to cn and hold in front, P3, K1 from cn, sl next 3 sts to cn and hold in back, K1, P3 from cn, P2, M1 pw, P2, 2 sts in cross-stitch rib, P3, 2 sts in little hourglass rib, P3, 2 sts in cross-stitch rib, P2, M1 pw, P2, sl next st to cn and hold in front, P3, K1 from cn, sl next 3 sts to cn and hold in back, K1, P3 from cn, P1f&b, K1 (2)—44 (46) sts.

Row 3: P1, K5 (6), P2, K8, P2, (K3, P2) twice, K8, P2, K5 (6), P1.

Cont in main patts and beg on row 12, inc 1 st at each edge (after and before selvage st) every 10 rows 4 times—52 (54) sts at end of row 42. Work even for 59 rows. Then beg on row 102, dec 1 st at each edge every 10 rows 4 times by using K1, P2tog tbl, work in patt to last 3 sts, P2tog, K1—44 (46) sts at end of row 142.

Row 143: Rep row 3.

Row 144 (RS): K1 (2), P2tog tbl, sl 3 sts to cn and hold in back, K1, K3 from cn, sl next st to cn, and hold in front, K3, K1 from cn, P3, P2tog tbl, 2 sts in cross-stitch rib, P3, 2 sts in little hourglass rib, P3, 2 sts in cross-stitch rib, P2tog, P3, sl next 3 sts to cn and hold in back, K1, K3 from cn, sl next st to cn and hold in front, K3, K1 from cn, P2tog, K1 (2)—40 (42) sts.

Row 145: P2tog tbl, K0 (1), P8, K4, P2, K3, P1, YO, P1, K3, P2, K4, P8, K0 (1), P2tog—39 (41) sts.

◆ Change to smaller needles. Returning to ribbing, work next row (RS) as follows: K2tog tbl, P6 (7), 2 sts in little hourglass rib, P3, 2 sts in cross-stitch rib, P3, 2 sts in little hourglass rib, P3, 2 sts in cross-stitch rib, P3, 2 sts in little hourglass rib, P6 (7), K2tog—36 (38) sts. Work dec on all RS rows as established in previous row for a total of 18 (20) rows. BO rem 20 sts.

Finishing

◆ Block pieces to measurements.

◆ Sew shoulder seams using invisible horizontal seaming (page 19).

◆ **Left front (button) band:** With smaller needles, PU from right to left 142 (147, 157, 162) sts.

Row 1 (WS): *P2, K3, rep from * to last 2 sts, P2.

Row 2: *2 sts in cross-stitch rib, P3, 2 sts in little hourglass rib, P3, rep from * to last 2 sts, work 2 sts in cross-stitch rib.

Rows 3 and 4: Work in established ribbing.

Row 5: Rep row 1.

Row 6: Rep row 2.

Next row: BO all sts in patt.

Evenly space desired number of buttons (10–12) and sew them in place.

◆ **Right front (buttonhole) band:** Work as for left front band through row 2.

Row 3: Work to beg of first buttonhole, turn and work row 4, turn and work row 5 and cut yarn. Attach yarn, work to next buttonhole and rep as for first, cut yarn.

Rep this process, evenly spacing button-holes to match placement of buttons. At end of row, turn and work row 6, joining all the separate sections. BO all sts in patt. Hand sew in whipstitch around buttonholes to secure.

✦ Sew sleeves into armholes using invisible vertical to horizontal seaming (page 19).

✦ Sew side seams and underarm seams using invisible vertical on reverse St st seaming (page 20).

✦ Place RS of collar against RS of cardigan, pinning evenly spaced and easing any full-ness. Use whipstitch (page 20) to sew these edges tog. Fold other long side of collar to inside and sew in place. Sew edges of collar closed.

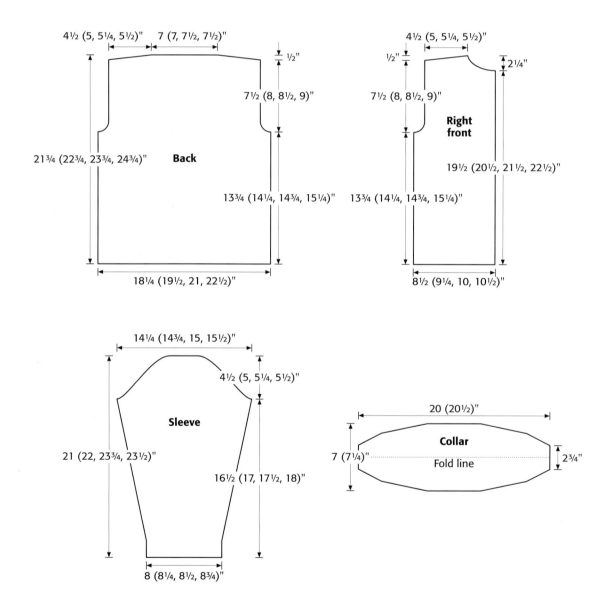

Triple Braided Diamonds Turtleneck

This sweater is a cable lover's dream,

rich with harmonious textures.

And if diamonds are a girl's best friend,

then this design certainly must be as well.

Skill Level:

■■■■

Materials

- 12 (13, 14, 15) skeins of Rowan Wool Cotton (50% wool, 50% cotton; 50 g; 123 yds), color 936 (③)
- Size 5 needles or size required to obtain gauge*
- Size 4 needles
- Size 4 circular needles (16")
- Cable needle

*3-needle BO requires 3 size 5 needles; third needle can be a straight needle or circular needles.

Gauge

28 sts and 26 rows = 4" in patt sts on size 5 needles when blocked

Size: Small (Medium, Large, Extra Large)

Finished Measurements

Bust: 34½ (37, 39, 41½)"

Length: 21½ (22½, 23½, 24½)"

Pattern Stitches

Triple Braided Diamonds

Multiple of 30 sts

FC (Front Cross) = sl 2 knit sts to cn and hold in front of work, P1, K2 from cn.

BC (Back Cross) = sl 1 purl st to cn and hold in back of work, K2, P1 from cn.

C4F (Cable 4 Front) = sl 2 sts to cn and hold in front of work, K2, K2 from cn.

C4B (Cable 4 Back) = sl 2 sts to cn and hold in back of work, K2, K2 from cn.

C6F (Cable 6 Front) = sl 3 sts to cn and hold in front of work, K3, K3 from cn.

C6B (Cable 6 Back) = sl 3 sts to cn and hold in back of work, K3, K3 from cn.

Row 1 (WS): K7, (P4, K2) twice, P4, K7.

Row 2: P6, (BC, FC) 3 times, P6.

Row 3 and all other WS rows: Knit all knit sts and purl all purl sts.

Row 4: P5, BC, (P2, C4B) twice, P2, FC, P5.

Row 6: P4, BC, P2, (BC, FC) twice, P2, FC, P4.

Row 8: P3, (BC, P2) twice, C4F, (P2, FC) twice, P3.

Row 10: (P2, BC) 3 times, (FC, P2) 3 times.

Rows 12, 14, and 16: Knit all knit sts and purl all purl sts.

Row 18: (P2, FC) 3 times, (BC, P2) 3 times.
Row 20: P3, (FC, P2) twice, C4F, (P2, BC) twice, P3.
Row 22: P4, FC, P2, (FC, BC) twice, P2, BC, P4.
Row 24: P5, FC, (P2, C4B) twice, P2, BC, P5.
Row 26: P6, (FC, BC) 3 times, P6.
Row 28: P7, (C4F, P2) twice, C4F, P7.
Rep these 28 rows for patt.

Seed Diamond and Cable

Multiple of 15 sts
C7B (Cable 7 Back) = sl 4 sts to cn and hold at back of work, K3, K4 from cn.
C7F (Cable 7 Front) = sl 3 sts to cn and hold at front of work, K4, K3 from cn.
T4R (Twist 4 Right) = sl next st to cn and hold at back of work, K3, P1 from cn.
T4L (Twist 4 Left) = sl 3 sts to cn and hold at front of work, P1, K3 from cn.

Row 1 (WS): K4, P7, K4.
Row 2: P4, C7B, P4 on right side of work (or P4, C7F, P4 on left side of work).
Row 3: Rep row 1.
Row 4: P3, T4R, P1, T4L, P3.
Row 5: K3, P3, K1, P1, K1, P3, K3.
Row 6: P2, T4R, K1, P1, K1, T4L, P2.
Row 7: K2, P3, (P1, K1) twice, P4, K2.
Row 8: P1, T4R, (P1, K1) twice, P1, T4L, P1.
Row 9: K1, P3, (K1, P1) 3 times, K1, P3, K1.
Row 10: T4R, (K1, P1) 3 times, K1, T4L.
Row 11: P3, (P1, K1) 4 times, P4.
Row 12: K3, (P1, K1) 4 times, P1, K3.
Row 13: Rep row 11.
Row 14: Rep row 12.
Row 15: Rep row 11.
Row 16: T4L, (K1, P1) 3 times, K1, T4R.
Row 17: Rep row 9.
Row 18: P1, T4L, (P1, K1) twice, P1, T4R, P1.
Row 19: Rep row 7.

Row 20: P2, T4L, K1, P1, K1, T4R, P2.
Row 21: Rep row 5.
Row 22: P3, T4L, P1, T4R, P3.
Row 23: Rep row 1.
Row 24: Rep row 2.
Row 25: Rep row 1.
Row 26: P4, K7, P4.
Row 27: Rep row 1.
Row 28: Rep row 26.
Rep these 28 rows for patt.

Seed Diamond

Multiple of 9 sts
C5B (Cable 5 Back) = sl 3 sts to cn and hold at back of work, K2, K3 sts from cn.
C5F (Cable 5 Front) = sl 2 sts to cn and hold at front of work, K3, K2 from cn.
T3B (Twist 3 Back) = sl next st to cn and hold at back of work, K2, P1 from cn.
T3F (Twist 3 Front) = sl 2 sts to cn and hold at front of work, P1, K2 from cn.

Row 1 (WS): K2, P5, K2.
Row 2: P2, C5B, P2 on right-hand side of work, (or P2, C5F, P2 on left-hand side of work).
Row 3: Rep row 1.
Row 4: P1, T3B, P1, T3F, P1.
Row 5: K1, P2, K1, P1, K1, P2, K1.
Row 6: T3B, K1, P1, K1, T3F.
Row 7: P2, (P1, K1) twice, P3.
Row 8: K2, (P1, K1) twice, P1, K2.
Row 9: P2, (P1, K1) twice, P3.
Row 10: Rep row 8.
Row 11: Rep row 9.
Row 12: T3F, K1, P1, K1, T3B.
Row 13: Rep row 5.
Row 14: P1, T3F, P1, T3B, P1.
Rep these 14 rows for patt.

Right Twist

Multiple of 2 sts

RT = K2tog leaving sts on left-hand needle, insert right-hand needle from the front between the 2 sts just knit tog and knit the first st again, then sl both sts from left- to right-hand needle.

Left Twist

Multiple of 2 sts

LT = With right-hand needle behind left-hand needle, skip 1 st and knit the 2nd st tbl, then insert right-hand needle into the back of both sts (skipped st and 2nd st) and K2tog tbl.

Back

♦ With smaller needles, cable CO 122 (130, 138, 146) sts and work bottom ribbing as follows:

Row 1 (WS): P1, K120 (128, 136, 144), P1.

Row 2: Purl.

Row 3: Rep row 1.

Row 4: Rep row 2.

Row 5: K1, P2 (0, 0, 2), K2 (2, 0, 2), *P4, K2*, rep from * to *, end P4, K2 (2, 0, 2), P2 (0, 0, 2), K1.

Row 6: K3 (1, 1, 3), P2 (2, 0, 2), *K4, P2*, rep from * to *, end K4, P2 (2, 0, 2), K3 (1, 1, 3).

Row 7: Rep row 5.

Row 8: K3 (1, 1, 3), P2 (2, 0, 2), *C4F, P2, K4, P2*, rep from * to *, end C4F, P2 (2, 0, 2), K3 (1, 1, 3).

Rows 9–24: Rep rows 5–8 another 4 times.

Row 25: Rep row 5.

Row 26: Knit all sts.

♦ Change to larger needles and establish main patts as follows:

Row 1 (WS): K2 (6, 7, 7), P2, K2, P4 (4, 4, 6), K2, P2, K2 (2, 3, 3), 15 sts in seed diamond with cable patt (row 1), K2 (2, 3, 3), P2, K2, P4 (4, 4, 6), K2, P2, K1 (1, 2, 2), 30 sts in triple braided diamonds patt (row 1), K1 (1, 2, 2), P2, K2, P4 (4, 4, 6), K2, P2, K2 (2, 3, 3), 15 sts in seed diamond with cable patt, K2 (2, 3, 3), P2, K2, P4 (4, 4, 6), K2, P2, K2 (6, 7, 7).

Row 2: K1, P1 (5, 6, 6), RT, P2, K4 (4, 4, 6), P2, LT, P2 (2, 3, 3), 15 sts in seed diamond with cable patt, P2 (2, 3, 3), RT, P2, K4 (4, 4, 6), P2, LT, P1 (1, 2, 2), 30 sts in triple braided diamonds patt, P1 (1, 2, 2), RT, P2, K4 (4, 4, 6), P2, LT, P2 (2, 3, 3), 15 sts in seed diamond with cable patt, P2 (2, 3, 3), RT, P2, K4 (4, 4, 6), P2, LT, P1 (5, 6, 6), K1.

Row 3: Knit all knit sts and purl all purl sts.

Row 4: K1, P1 (5, 6, 6), RT, P2, C4F (C4F, C4F, C6F), P2, LT, P2 (2, 3, 3), 15 sts in seed diamond with cable patt, P2 (2, 3, 3), RT, P2, C4B (C4B, C4B, C6B), P2, LT, P1 (1, 2, 2), 30 sts in triple braided diamonds patt, P1 (1, 2, 2), RT, P2, C4F (C4F, C4F, C6F), P2, LT, P2 (2, 3, 3), 15 sts in seed diamond with cable patt, P2

(2, 3, 3), RT, P2, C4B (C4B, C4B, C6B), P2, LT, P1 (5, 6, 6), K1. Work C4F (C4F, C4F, C6F) and C4B (C4B, C4B, C6B) every sixth row from this point on, such as row 10, 16, 22, and so on.

Cont in main patts until work measures 20¼ (21¼, 22¼, 23¼)" from beg.

- ✦ Shape neck: Work in patt across 49 (51, 53, 55) sts, attach 2nd ball of yarn and BO center 24 (28, 32, 36) sts, finish row. Working both sides at same time with 2 separate balls of yarn, at beg of each neck edge on EOR, dec 1 st, then BO 6 sts once, dec 1 st, then BO 3 sts once, dec 1 st, then BO 1 st once—36 (38, 40, 42) sts for each shoulder. Place sts on stitch holders.

Front

- ✦ Work as for back until 19¼ (20¼, 21¼, 22¼)" from beg.
- ✦ Shape neck: Work in patt across 49 (51, 53, 55) sts, attach 2nd ball of yarn and BO center 24 (28, 32, 36) sts, finish row. Working both sides at same time with 2 separate balls of yarn, at beg of each neck edge on EOR, dec 1 st, then BO 5 sts once, dec 1 st, then BO 2 sts once, dec 1 st, then BO 1 st once, dec 1 st 2 times—36 (38, 40, 42) sts for each shoulder.
- ✦ Work 5 rows even and place shoulder sts on st holders.

Sleeves

- ✦ With smaller needles, cable CO 56 (56, 62, 62) sts and work ribbing as follows:
  Row 1 (WS): P1, K54 (54, 60, 60), P1.
  Row 2: Purl.
  Row 3: Rep row 1.

Row 4: Rep row 2.

Row 5: K2, *P4, K2*, rep from * to *.

Row 6: K1, P1, *K4, P2*, rep from * to *, end K4, P1, K1.

Row 7: Rep row 5.

Row 8: K1, P1, *C4F, P2, K4, P2*, rep from * to *, end C4F, P1, K1 for Small and Medium; end C4F, P2, K4, P1, K1 for Large and Extra Large.

Rows 9–20: Rep rows 5–8 another 3 times.

Row 21: Rep row 5.

✦ Change to larger needles.

Next row: K1, *M1 kw, K7 (7, 8, 8)*, rep from * to * 2 times, **M1 kw, K6**, rep from ** to ** 1 time, ***M1 kw, K7 (7, 8, 8)***, rep from *** to *** 2 times, end M1 kw, K1—65 (65, 71, 71) sts.

✦ Establish main patts as follows:

Note: *Until inc on row 6, sizes Small (S) and Medium (M) will have only 8 sts in seed diamond st. For rows 1, 2, and 4, work these 8 sts as indicated in italics for S and M.*

- **Row 1 (WS):** K1 (1, 3, 3), work 8 (8, 9, 9) sts in seed diamond patt *(for S and M work as K1, P5, K2)*, K2, P2, K2, P4, K2, P2, K2, work 15 sts in seed diamond with cable patt, K2, P2, K2, P4, K2, P2, K2, work 8 (8, 9, 9) sts in seed diamond patt *(for S and M work as K2, P5, K1)*, K1 (1, 3, 3).
- **Row 2:** K1, P0 (0, 2, 2), work 8 (8, 9, 9) sts in seed diamond patt *(for S and M work as P1, C5B, P2)*, P2, RT, P2, K4, P2, LT, P2, work 15 sts in seed diamond with cable patt, P2, RT, P2, K4, P2, LT, P2, work 8 (8, 9, 9) sts in seed diamond patt *(for S and M work as P2, C5F, P1)*, P0 (0, 2, 2), K1.
- **Row 3:** Rep row 1.
- **Row 4:** K1, P0 (0, 2, 2), work 8 (8, 9, 9) sts in seed diamond patt *(for S and M work as T3B, P1, T3F, P1)*, P2, RT, P2, C4B, P2, LT, P2, work 15 sts in seed diamond with cable patt, P2, RT, P2, C4F, P2, LT, P2, work 8 (8, 9, 9) sts in seed diamond patt *(for S and M work as P1, T3B, P1, T3F)*, P0 (0, 2, 2), K1. Note that you will work C4B and C4F every 6 rows.

✦ Cont in established main patts, inc 1 st each edge beg on row 6 by using M1 kw or pw as appropriate between first 2 sts at beg and end of row. Work this inc every 6 rows a total of 15 times—95 (95, 101, 101) sts. Work same inc every 7 rows a total of 4 (4, 6, 6) times—103 (103, 113, 113) sts.

- When work measures approx 19 (19, 21, 21)", and ending with row 14 (14, 26, 26) of seed diamond with cable patt, place sleeve sts on st holder.

Finishing

- Opening up work, block front, back, and sleeves to measurements. To block sts on holders, place sts on strand of contrasting yarn by threading yarn needle through sts on holders. To maintain the slightly ruffled look, do not block the 4 rows of garter edging that create the border on the back, front, and cuffs. Simply begin pinning to block above these borders. Do not block the turtleneck. After blocking, place sts on size 5 needles in preparation for 3-needle BO.
- Use 3-needle BO for shoulder seams (page 21).
- For sleeves, place markers over 14¾ (14¾, 16, 16)" on front and back side edges with shoulder seam at center and with size 5 needles PU 103 (103, 113, 113) sts between markers. Use 3-needle BO to seam sleeves to front and back.
- Sew side seams and underarm seams using invisible vertical on reverse St st seaming (page 20).
- **Turtleneck:** With smaller circular needles, and beg at shoulder seam, PU 120 (120, 132, 132) sts along neck edge. Purl 3 rnds. **Next rnd:** *P2, K4*, rep from * to * for 3 rnds; try to center a K4 at front of neckline. On every 4th rnd work alternating K4 as C4F as for cuff and front and back edging. Work approx 22 rnds in this manner knowing you may want to work more rnds in this patt if you have a long neck or like a higher turtleneck. End with 3 rnds of purl, then BO pw on next rnd, working P2tog 10 times evenly spaced for better neck edge.

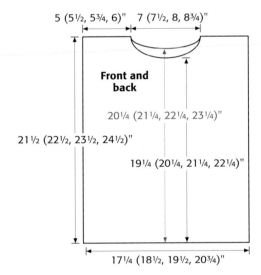

5 (5½, 5¾, 6)"   7 (7½, 8, 8¾)"

Front and back

20¼ (21¼, 22¼, 23¼)"

21½ (22½, 23½, 24½)"

19¼ (20¼, 21¼, 22¼)"

17¼ (18½, 19½, 20¾)"

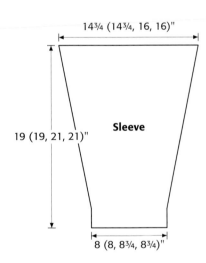

14¾ (14¾, 16, 16)"

Sleeve

19 (19, 21, 21)"

8 (8, 8¾, 8¾)"

Textural appeal is at its peak in the
Lily of the Valley Cardigan. This fitted sweater
may require patience, but the result
will be enormously rewarding and well worth
your efforts. I have to say I loved knitting
every stitch and can assure you that you will
grow to love bobbles if you make this sweater.
The theme is nature—flowers and leaves,
curved lines, and open spaces. The feeling
is soft, flattering, and definitely feminine.
The sleeves are bracelet length.

Skill Level:

Note: *This sweater is blocked to the measurements on the schematic. Because of the density of the texture in this pattern and mercerized cotton's tendency to hold its shape, you will possibly lose approximately 1½" in cardigan width after blocking and seaming.*

Materials

+ 9 (10, 11, 12) balls of Jaeger Siena 4 Ply (100% mercerized cotton; 50g; 153 yds), color 405 **(1)**
+ Size 4 needles (14" straight or 36" circular) or size required to obtain gauge
+ Size 4 dpn

Size: Petite (Small, Medium, Large)
Finished Measurements
Bust: 36¾ (38¼, 40, 42)"
Length: 21 (21½, 23, 23½)"

Gauge

24 sts and 30 rows = 4" in patt sts when blocked

Pattern Stitches

Mimosa Border

Multiple of 26 plus 1

MB (make bobble) = K1f&b&f of same st; turn and K3; turn and P3; turn and K3; turn and K3tog. Purl into back of this st on next WS row.

Rows 1 and 3 (WS): K27.

Row 2: P27.

Row 4: P1, K25, P1.

Rows 5, 7, 9, 11, 13, 15, and 17: K1, P25, K1.

Row 6: P1 (K1, YO) twice, K7, SSK, sl 1, K2tog, psso, K2tog, K7, (YO, K1) twice, K1.

Row 8: P1, K2, YO, K1, YO, K2, MB, K3, SSK, sl 1, K2tog, psso, K2tog, K3, MB, K2, YO, K1, YO, K2, P1.

Row 10: P1, MB, K2, YO, K1, YO, K2, MB, K2, SSK, sl 1, K2tog, psso, K2tog, K2, MB, K2, YO, K1, YO, K2, MB, P1.

Row 12: P1, K1, MB, K2, YO, K1, YO, K2, MB, K1, SSK, sl 1, K2tog, psso, K2tog, K1, MB, K2, YO, K1, YO, K2, MB, K1, P1.

Row 14: P1, K2, MB, K2, YO, K1, YO, K2, MB, SSK, sl 1, K2tog, psso, K2tog, MB, K2, YO, K1, YO, K2, MB, K2, P1.

Row 16: P1, K3, MB, K2, YO, K1, YO, K2, SSK, sl 1, K2tog, psso, K2tog, K2, YO, K1, YO, K2, MB, K3, P1.

Row 18: Rep row 4.

Rows 19, 20, and 21: Rep rows 1, 2, and 3.

Twin Leaf Panel

Multiple of 10 sts

SSK and pass = SSK, return the resulting st to left-hand needle and with point of right-hand needle pass the next st over it and off needle, sl the st back to the right-hand needle.

Twin Leaf Panel Slanting Right

Row 1 and all WS rows: P10.
Row 2: K6, SSK and pass, YO, K1, YO.
Row 4: K4, SSK and pass, K1, YO, K1, YO, K1.
Row 6: K2, SSK and pass, K2, YO, K1, YO, K2.
Row 8: SSK and pass, K3, YO, K1, YO, K3.
Rep these 8 rows for patt.

Twin Leaf Panel Slanting Left

Row 1 and all WS rows: P10.
Row 2: YO, K1, YO, sl 1, K2tog, psso, K6.
Row 4: K1, YO, K1, YO, K1, sl 1, K2tog, psso, K4.
Row 6: K2, YO, K1, YO, K2, sl 1, K2tog, psso, K2.
Row 8: K3, YO, K1, YO, K3, sl 1, K2tog, psso.
Rep these 8 rows for patt.

Lily of the Valley

Multiple of 23 sts

MB = K1f&b&f of same st; turn and K3; turn and P3; turn and K3; turn and K3tog. Purl into back of this st on next WS row.

Row 1 and all WS rows: P23.
Row 2: SSK, K6, YO, K1, YO, K1, sl 1, K2tog, psso, K1, YO, K1, YO, K6, K2tog.
Row 4: SSK, K5, YO, K1, YO, K2, sl 1, K2tog, psso, K2, YO, K1, YO, K5, K2tog.
Row 6: SSK, K4, YO, K1, YO, MB, K2, sl 1, K2tog, psso, K2, MB, YO, K1, YO, K4, K2tog.
Row 8: SSK, K3, YO, K1, YO, MB, K3, sl 1, K2tog, psso, K3, MB, YO, K1, YO, K3, K2tog.
Row 10: SSK, K2, YO, K1, YO, MB, K4, sl 1, K2tog, psso, K4, MB, YO, K1, YO, K2, K2tog.
Row 12: SSK, K1, YO, K1, YO, MB, K5, sl 1, K2tog, psso, K5, MB, YO, K1, YO, K1, K2tog.
Row 14: SSK, YO, K1, YO, MB, K6, sl 1, K2tog, psso, K6, MB, YO, K1, YO, K2tog.
Rep these 14 rows for patt.

Back

✦ Cable CO 107 (112, 117, 122) sts and work mimosa border as follows:
Row 1 and all WS rows: P1 (selvage st), K105 (110, 115, 120), P1 (selvage st).
Row 2: K1, P105 (110, 115, 120), K1.

Row 4: K1, P1 (2, 3, 4), *K25, P1 (2, 3, 4)*, rep from * to * 3 times, K1.

Row 6: K1, P1 (2, 3, 4), *K1, YO, K1, YO, K7, SSK, sl 1, K2tog, psso, K2tog, K7, YO, K1, YO, K1, P1 (2, 3, 4)*, rep from * to * 3 times, K1.

Row 8: K1, P1 (2, 3, 4), *K2, YO, K1, YO, K2, MB, K3, SSK, sl 1, K2tog, psso, K2tog, K3, MB, K2, YO, K1, YO, K2, P1 (2, 3, 4)*, rep from * to * 3 times, K1.

Row 10: K1, P1 (2, 3, 4), *MB, K2, YO, K1, YO, K2, MB, K2, SSK, sl 1, K2tog, psso, K2tog, K2, MB, K2, YO, K1, YO, K2, MB, P1 (2, 3, 4)*, rep from * to * 3 times, K1.

Row 12: K1, P1 (2, 3, 4), *K1, MB, K2, YO, K1, YO, K2, MB, K1, SSK, sl 1, K2tog, psso, K2tog, K1, MB, K2, YO, K1, YO, K2, MB, K1, P1 (2, 3, 4)*, rep from * to * 3 times, K1.

Row 14: K1, P1 (2, 3, 4), *K2, MB, K2, YO, K1, YO, K2, MB, SSK, sl 1, K2tog, psso, K2tog, MB, K2, YO, K1, YO, K2, MB, K2, P1 (2, 3, 4)*, rep from * to * 3 times, K1.

Row 16: K1, P1 (2, 3, 4), *K3, MB, K2, YO, K1, YO, K2, SSK, sl 1, K2tog, psso, K2tog, K2, YO, K1, YO, K2, MB, K3, P1 (2, 3, 4)*, rep from * to * 3 times, K1.

Row 18: Rep row 4.

Rows 19, 20, and 21: Rep rows 1, 2, and 3.

+ **Transition row: (RS):** K1, P1 (1, 3, 5), K10, P2 (3, 3, 3), K23, P2 (3, 3, 3), K10, P2 (3, 3, 4), K2, M1 kw 0 (1, 0, 1) times, K3 (2, 3, 2), P2 (3, 3, 4), K10, P2 (3, 3, 3), K23, P2 (3, 3, 3), K10, P1 (1, 3, 5), K1—107 (113, 117, 123) sts.

+ Establish main patts as follows:

Row 1 (WS): P1, K1 (1, 3, 5), P10, K2 (3, 3, 3), P23, K2 (3, 3, 3), P10, K2 (3, 3, 4), P5, K2 (3, 3, 4), P10, K2 (3, 3, 3), P23, K2 (3, 3, 3), P10, K1 (1, 3, 5), P1.

Row 2 (RS): K1, P1 (1, 3, 5), 10 sts in right slant twin leaf patt (row 2), P2 (3, 3, 3), 23 sts in lily of the valley patt (row 2), P2 (3, 3, 3), 10 sts in left slant twin leaf patt, P2 (3, 3, 4), SSK, YO, K1, YO, K2tog (last 5 sts will be worked in same way every RS row), P2 (3, 3, 4), 10 sts in right slant twin leaf patt, P2 (3, 3, 3), 23 sts in lily of the valley patt, P2 (3, 3, 3), 10 sts in left slant twin leaf patt, P1 (1, 3, 5), K1.

Cont in established main patts through row 82 (82, 90, 90). Work will measure approx 13¾ (13¾, 14¾, 14¾)" from beg.

+ **Shape armholes:** BO 3 (3, 3, 4) sts at beg of next 2 rows. Dec 1 st, then BO 1 (1, 2, 2) sts at beg of next 2 rows. Note that decs in twin leaf patt will lead into same patt as center 5 sts on RS, which will be K1, P1, SSK, YO, K1, YO, K2tog on right side of back and SSK, YO, K1, YO, K2tog, P1, K1 on left side of back. On WS rows these 5 sts will be P5— 97 (103, 105, 109) sts rem. Cont until arm-hole measures 6¾ (7¼, 7¾, 8¼)".

+ **Shape shoulders:** BO 9 (10, 10, 11) sts at beg of next 2 rows. Dec 1 st, then BO 9 (10, 10, 11) sts at beg of next 2 rows. Dec 1 st, then BO 11 sts at beg of next 2 rows. Place rem 35 (37, 39, 39) sts on holder to work later for neck edging. Note that shoulder decs will vary slightly as patt will reduce some sts by omitting YO in row before BO occurs. Twin leaf patt may become plain St st in last few rows approaching neckline edge.

Front

Directions are written for right front. Remember to reverse armhole, neck, and shoulder shaping for left front.

+ Cable CO 57 (59, 62, 65) sts and work mimosa border patt as follows:

    Row 1 and 3 (WS): P1, K55 (57, 60, 63), P1.

    Row 2: K1, P55 (57, 60, 63), K1.

    Row 4: K1, P2 (2, 3, 4), *K25, P1 (2, 3, 4)*, rep from * to * 1 time, P1, K1.

    Rows 5–21: Cont patt as established.

+ **Transition row (RS):** K1, P1 (1, 3, 5), K10, P4 (5, 5, 5), K23, P4 (5, 5, 5), K10, P3 (3, 4, 5), K1.

+ Establish main patts as follows:

    Row 1 (WS): P1, K3 (3, 4, 5), P10, K4 (5, 5, 5), P23, K4 (5, 5, 5), P10, K1 (1, 3, 5), P1.

    Row 2: K1, P1 (1, 3, 5), 10 sts in right slant twin leaf patt (row 2), P4 (5, 5, 5), 23 sts in lily of the valley patt (row 2), P4 (5, 5, 5), 10 sts in left slant twin leaf patt (remember to reverse left slant and right slant on left front), P3 (3, 4, 5), K1.

+ Cont in established patts shaping armhole and shoulders as for back. AT SAME TIME shape neckline when work measures 18½ (19, 20½, 21)". At neck edge, BO 8 (8, 9, 9) sts once. Dec 1 st, then BO 3 (3, 4, 4) sts once. Dec 1 st, then BO 2 sts once. Dec 1 st, then BO 1 st once. Dec 1 st 4 times.

Sleeves

+ Cable CO 57 (59, 62, 65) sts and work mimosa border patt, transition row and establish main patts as for front. Starting on row 6 (3, 6, 6) of main patts, inc 1 st each edge between selvage st and next st by using M1 pw on RS and M1 kw on WS every 6 rows 16 (17, 17, 18) times—89 (93, 96, 101) sts. Work even for 2 (3, 4, 2) more rows. Sleeve will measure approx 15 (15½, 16, 16½)".

+ **Shape cap:** BO 3 (3, 4, 4) sts at beg of next 2 rows. Dec 1 st, then BO 1 (1, 2, 3) sts at beg of next 2 rows. Dec 1 st each edge EOR 0 (1, 4, 10) times. Dec 1 st each edge next 19 (20, 18, 9) rows. Dec 1 st, then BO 3 (3, 1, 3) sts at beg of next 2 rows. Dec 1 st, then BO 4 (3, 2, 3) sts beg of next 2 rows. BO rem 23 (25, 28, 31) sts.

Finishing

+ Block pieces to measurements, opening up pattern and sts as you pin for blocking. Note that when pinning and blocking, you must make an effort to clearly establish vertical and horizontal lines in patts.

+ Sew shoulder seams using invisible horizontal seaming (page 19).

+ Sew sleeve into armhole edge using invisible vertical to horizontal seaming (page 19).

+ Sew side seams and sleeve seams using invisible vertical on reverse St st seaming (page 20).

+ **Front edges:** With 36" circular needle, PU 114 (116, 124, 128) along one front edge at a time. With dpn, cable CO 4 sts and work I-cord using one of picked up edge sts at a time as 5th st to form I-cord edge (page 16). BO last 5 sts.

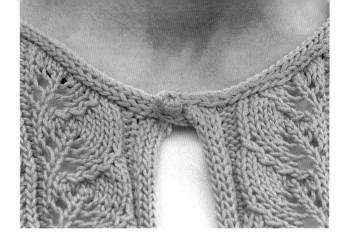

Neck edging: With 14" circular needles, PU 30 (30, 34, 34) sts, move 35 (37, 39, 39) sts from holder at back neck to needle, PU 30 (30, 34, 34) sts at rem of neck edge. With dpn, cable CO 2 sts and work 12 rows I-cord and tie in a knot to create bobble-type button. Cable CO 2 more sts and work I-cord around neck edge. BO 2 sts and work 12 rows of I-cord. BO rem 2 sts and use last 12 rows to create a loop for a buttonhole. Sew end of loop securely in place. Note that I-cord button will resemble a bobble and could be replaced with a traditional button of your choice as long as the I-cord loop for closure was the appropriate length for your chosen button.

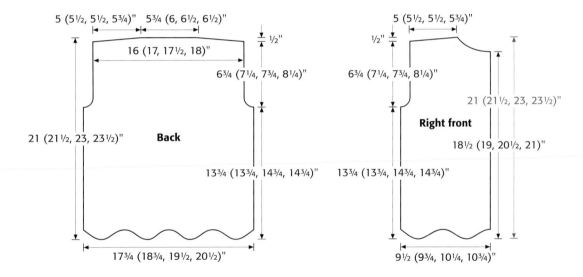

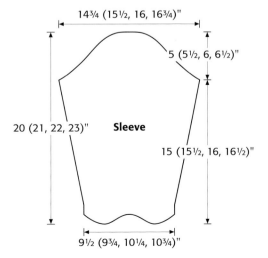

Bibliography

Vogue Knitting. New York: Pantheon Books, 1989.

Burmeister, Alice, and Tom Monte. *The Touch of Healing.* New York: Bantam Books, 1997.

Johnson, Will. *The Posture of Meditation: A Practical Guide for Meditators of All Traditions.* Boston: Shambala Publications, 1996.

Walker, Barbara G. *A Treasury of Knitting Patterns.* Pittsville, WI.: Schoolhouse Press Edition, 1998.

Walker, Barbara G. *A Second Treasury of Knitting Patterns.* Pittsville, WI.: Schoolhouse Press Edition, 1998.

Wiseman, Nancy M. *The Knitter's Book of Finishing Techniques.* Woodinville, WA.: Martingale & Company, 2002.

Resources

Contact the following companies to find shops that carry the yarns in this book.

Sesia
The Red Needle
Mickey Landau
1711 E. Victory Dr.
Savannah, GA 31404
912-691-1071
Sesia Cable 2005

Sandnes
www.awesomeewe.com
Mandarin Petit

Bernat
www.bernat.com
Bernat Handicrafter Cotton

Brown Sheep Yarns
www.brownsheep.com
Nature Spun Fingering

Cascade Yarn
www.cascadeyarns.com
Sierra

Debbie Bliss
www.debbiebliss.freeserve.co.uk
Wool/Cotton

Elann
www.elann.com
Endless Summer Collection Sonata

Jaeger
www.royalyarns.com
www.theknittinggarden.com
Baby Merino 4 ply
Siena 4 Ply

Knit One, Crochet Too
www.knitonecrochettoo.com
Madelaine

Plymouth Yarns
www.plymouthyarn.com
Fantasy Naturale

Ram Wools
www.ramwools.com
Mandarin Petit

Rowan
www.knitrowan.com
Wool/Cotton
Cotton Glace
4 Ply Cotton

S.R. Kertzer
www.kertzer.com
Butterfly Super 10

Tahki Yarns
www.tahkistacycharles.com
Cotton Classic
Willow